A Collector's Guide to

Costume Jewelry

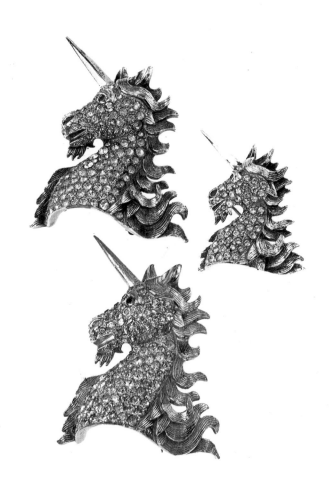

A Collector's Guide to

Costume Jewelry

KEY STYLES AND HOW TO
RECOGNIZE THEM

TRACY TOLKIEN AND HENRIETTA WILKINSON

FIREFLY BOOKS

A FIREFLY BOOK

First published in Canada in 1997
by Firefly Books Ltd.
3680 Victoria Park Avenue
Willowdale, Ontario M2H 3K1

Canadian Cataloguing in Publication Data

Tolkien, Tracy, 1962-
          A collector's guide to costume jewelry. Key styles and how to
recognize them.

ISBN 1-55209-156-2
1. Costume jewelry   Collectors and collecting.
2. Costume jewelry - History. I. Wilkinson, Henrietta, 1960-
II. Title.

NK4890.C67T64 1997   688'.2'075   C97 930883-6

Senior editors Tom Whyte, Marilyn Inglis
Copy editors Elizabeth Ingles, Maggi McCormick
Designer Paul Hetherington
Design assistant Sabine Heitz
Photographer Michael Harvey
Picture researcher Zoe Holtermann
Editorial director Gilly Cameron Cooper
Art director Moira Clinch
Assistant art director Penny Cobb

Typeset in Great Britain by
Central Southern Typesetters, Eastbourne
Manufactured in Singapore by Bright Arts (Singapore) Pte Ltd
Printed in Singapore by Star Standard Industries (Pte) Ltd

Contents

Introduction

What we think of today as costume jewelry has a long history, stretching right back to the time of our earliest ancestors. Just like contemporary jewelers, they lavished care and attention on material that was turned into decorative jewelry, creating finely worked objects out of everyday materials such as bone or discarded shell. Today, as always, costume jewelry is regarded as separate from more valuable jewels, which are clear declarations of their wearer's status. But despite the fact that costume jewelry has always been made from nonprecious materials, much of it is as intrinsically beautiful as its precious equivalent. Its originality of design and quality of workmanship have insured that costume jewelry has an important place in the history of personal adornment.

The term "costume jewelry" is a 20th-century invention, generally referring to jewelry pieces that were designed to accompany a specific outfit or a current style. Since fashion is by its very nature transient, and often whimsical, so too was, and is, much costume jewelry, which was never intended to be treasured in the same way as valuable jewels, or as mementos with sentimental value. On the contrary, costume jewelry is often flamboyant and eccentric, made to amuse, to be worn and enjoyed, rather than kept carefully in a safe place.

The development of the haute couture trade, which began at the end of the 19th century creating individual fashions for the very wealthy, was instrumental in establishing costume jewelry as a distinct category of its own, especially once leading 20th-century couture designers, such as the legendary Coco Chanel, came to the fore. Consequently, the term is most often taken to refer to the modernist jewelry of the Art Deco and subsequent years, through the 1920s, 30s, 40s, and 50s. Because the skills employed by 20th-century costume jewelers owed much to the work of earlier craftsmen, this book also looks back at jewels made from non- and semiprecious

After World War II there was a strong move toward a more glamorous style in fashion and in costume jewelry. The Trifari paste and amber earrings from the early 1950s (*above*) reflect the move away from austerity that prevailed at that time. Butler & Wilson, London.

French Art Deco compacts decorated with very popular motifs from the 1920s. Christopher St. James, Ritzy, London.

Micromosaic jewelry such as the necklace, *c.* 1860 (*left*) began to appear shortly after the discovery of Classical ruins in Greece and Italy. Many jewelers sought to imitate ancient arts in jewelry-making. Beauty & the Beasts, London.

Trifari is one of the most significant names in costume jewelry, and the above two pieces are typical of its designs in the 1950s. First Lady Mamie Eisenhower commissioned Trifari to design pieces for the Presidential inaugurations in 1952 and 1956.

materials in the preceding two centuries. In the 18th century, a passion for true gemstones led to a search for the ultimate in imitation stones made of glass, beginning the process that has led to today's flourishing industry in cut glass gems, while the search for an alternative to expensive gold resulted in the earliest gilt metals.

As working with these glass stones and gold substitutes allowed jewelers the freedom to experiment in a way that would never have been possible with precious metals and gems, a vast range of interesting and unique jewels was being made by the late 19th century. Other nonprecious materials used to create these pieces included iron, steel, hair, and even the earliest plastics.

The 19th century, a time of profound change in Europe, saw the widespread adoption of industrial methods of production. For the first time ever, jewelry of mass appeal, turned out by the new machine-run industries, was affordable by all, and the idea that jewelry was for everyone, not just the rich, was born. It was a short step from here to the glass- and plastic-dominated costume jewelry of the 20th century.

Much of the earliest paste jewelry was produced to imitate precious jewels, and ladies would wear the fakes while their valuable pieces remained safely locked up. The beautiful graduated white paste trefoil necklace, *c.* 1875, (*above*) glitters as magnificently as one made of diamonds. Harvey & Gore, London.

Luckily for the collector, the lack of inherent value in this earliest costume jewelry, that of the 18th and 19th centuries, meant that many pieces avoided the fate of their more precious counterparts of being melted down or reworked. Never the less, although 18th-century paste is still available, the amount is dwindling rapidly as collectors snap up those pieces in good condition that appear on the market. Jewelry from the 19th century, and especially the latter part, is still very collectible, partly because of the quantities manufactured thanks to mass production, and partly because it was a time of experimentation. Jewelry was produced in every conceivable style and in a wide range of materials, and collectors have come to prize even the humblest of 19th-century jewels for the quality of their workmanship.

Both early and more recent costume jewelry does, on occasion, combine precious and nonprecious materials, which makes the distinction between

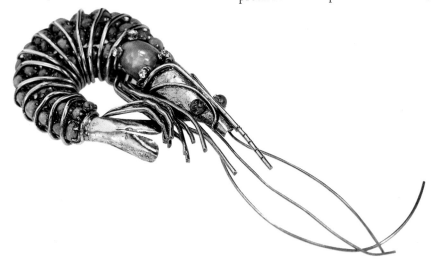

Contemporary costume jewelry designer Iradj Moini creates dramatic pieces that are complete one-offs using uncut pastes in wire frames. Jewels such as this shrimp are handmade and will take him up to two weeks to complete. As a result, his work is expensive but instantly collectible. Diane Keith, Beverly Hills.

precious jewelry, "art" jewels (which pushed back the boundaries of design), and costume jewelry sometimes difficult to define. Precious jewelry, in which all or almost all of the materials used, such as gold, diamonds, pearls, or gemstones, are considered valuable in their own right, is clearly not costume jewelry. Art jewels produced by such designers as René Lalique, Louis Comfort Tiffany, and Georg Jensen, can be more problematic, however, as they were often made with a varied mix of materials: glass with emeralds, chrome with platinum. But on the whole, such jewels are not held to be costume jewelry, as they were works of great originality, almost always one-off pieces.

In many cases, art jewels were highly influential and inspired countless pieces that could truly be called costume. Top-ranking jewelry designers often ran companies that turned out more downscale versions of their original designs, that sold for very low prices. Changes in taste and appreciation over the years can cause the value of such pieces to increase out of all proportion. Glass pendants made by René Lalique's firm in the first years of the 20th century are a good example. They were made in their thousands and sold very cheaply, but fetch infinitely more now as collectors push up their prices.

On the whole, costume jewelry means pieces which are made primarily from nonprecious materials, of which silver is considered one, and which were produced in large enough quantities to make them available to more than just the élite. This open-ended definition has one great advantage for collectors: it can include almost anything that takes their fancy, especially pieces that date from the eclectic 19th century and before. As in all areas of collecting, the important thing is to buy pieces that please rather than those which look like sure-fire investments: fashions change on a whim, and what might be highly collectible today may be forgotten tomorrow.

The seemingly Art Deco brooch (*above*) is, in fact, a very good modern reproduction of that particular style and illustrates the Deco trend toward flattened, geometric shapes. Steven Miners, Cristobal, London.

9

COLLECTING

Most costume jewelry collections start with a chance encounter. An attractive bracelet catches your eye at a fleamarket. It costs very little, so you buy it for fun and end up wearing it constantly. Next, you see a pair of earrings in an antique store window that match your bracelet perfectly. These are 1940s Miriam Haskell originals, and the dealer shows you that your fleamarket find is signed by Haskell as well and is therefore a real bargain. By now, of course you're hooked! But how do you turn this spark into an organized, coherent collection?

At this stage you should actually stop buying jewelry, and spend some time learning, looking, and thinking. The worst mistakes are made when enthusiasm is keen but knowledge is still very sketchy. Restraint is difficult, but worth it. Your initial research should center on books: reference and special studies of particular areas. Familiarize yourself with the look of various periods and designers, and make a list of those that appeal. This list might be wildly eclectic but there is nothing wrong with that, because part of the fun and excitement of collecting costume jewelry lies in its infinite variety. Every purchase can be an exercise of personal style and taste. Armed with a bit of information and at least some idea of what you want to focus on, your next step is to look — to visit every dealer, antique market or center, and museum you can find.

This gives you a chance to pinpoint the dealers whose taste most closely parallels your own. The best collections are formed through collaboration with a few favorite dealers, because they get to know you and what you are after. This relationship will prove particularly valuable if and when you reach the stage of trying to fill specific gaps in your collection, at which point a list can be given to your dealers who can look out for items for you. This sort of partnership is also vital for the repairs which become inevitable if you choose, as you should do, to wear your costume jewelry. There will always be fleamarkets, garage sales, and one-off finds, but the cornerstone of a comprehensive collection is usually a dealer/customer relationship.

Ways of Collecting

There are many ways of collecting costume jewelry. Some collectors like to form wide-ranging, wearable collections of reasonably priced items geared to their wardrobes and style preferences, while others prefer to concentrate their resources on a few spectacular showpieces. You might focus on a theme, such as baskets, bows, or animals, and buy appealing examples from all areas. You might prefer to limit your collection to a particular period. Many collectors of 20th-century costume jewelry enjoy acquiring pieces by a particular designer such as Miriam Haskell, or Trifari, while others like to spread their net much wider. All these approaches are valid. The only hard and fast rule in collecting may seem obvious, but should always be kept in mind, and that is, quite simply, *only to buy pieces that you like*. While the value of

Bakelite and brass frog brooch. The 1988 sale of Andy Warhol's Bakelite collection sent demand for Bakelite through the roof. The best pieces are now extremely rare and prices are correspondingly high. Christopher St. James, Ritzy, London.

A collection of face brooches, *c.* 1890–1970. Some collectors concentrate on themes such as butterflies, baskets, or bows, and these might date from the 18th century to the present, spanning a wide variety of styles and materials. Specific themes can be worn singly or combined into eclectic groups. Steinberg & Tolkien, London.

costume jewelry can appreciate quite sharply, it is not an area in which purely financial investments should be made, because fashion fads can distort prices and the market is relatively new and specialized.

The *Jewels of Fantasy* traveling exhibition (1991–93) sponsored by the Swarovski Crystal Company did an enormous amount to raise 20th-century costume jewelry from a 1980s fashion trend into a legitimate area for the serious collector. Its comprehensive catalogue brought together a wealth of valuable information on the subject.

Costume jewelry still has not managed to shake off its association with precious materials altogether, but many people are surprised by how valuable it can be. It is worth remembering that the so-called intrinsic value of, for example, a small, modern 18kt gold ring with tiny diamond chips will amount to only a fraction of its retail price. Indifferently designed, low-quality jewelry, be it costume or precious, has no real investment potential. The value of an elaborate, interesting piece by Miriam Haskell bought in the early 1980s has appreciated quite considerably, while most run-of-the-mill precious jewelry has not. People who bought boring, low-quality period costume jewelry during the retro boom in the mid-1980s have lost money.

Period costume jewelry often has unexpected, unfamiliar features. This rhinestone brooch (*above*) comes apart and can be worn as two separate clips. The central panel of the Bakelite bracelet (*above right*) opens to reveal a hidden powder puff and mirror which is flanked by two tiny lipstick holders. Tessa Innes, London.

When you are shopping for costume jewelry, keep your eyes open for pieces which complement your existing collection. Diane Keith purchased these fish separately but found that they now make a fantastic impression when all three are worn together. Diane Keith, Beverly Hills.

Now that the market has stabilized, prices are much more realistic, but as with any antique, fine rare examples will always rise steadily in value while lesser examples will fluctuate with the fickleness of fashion.

Sources for the Novice

Specialist dealers and auction houses are good, reliable sources for the novice collector, and are often the best sources overall for rare, important pieces. If a question of authenticity arises, you can return your purchase and expect a full refund. This should, in theory, also be true of goods purchased at a fair or market, but it often proves impossible to trace the dealer, or to establish that you bought the item in good faith as an original. Wherever you buy period costume jewelry, always ask for a receipt stating the approximate age and, if applicable, the designer of each piece.

Once you feel protected by your own knowledge it's well worth branching out to some of the less obvious sources of costume jewelry, where real bargains can be had. While a general dealer at a fleamarket or show may overprice a mediocre piece because it happens to be signed by a designer, he or she could equally well underprice a spectacular and rare example by the same designer. Some general dealers do not rate costume jewelry and lump it all together in their junk baskets. Both the advantages and the pitfalls of collection always revolve around specialized knowledge.

Vintage clothing stores can be a good source of bargains. They tend to cater for young people on budgets, and fancy-dress customers, so the period jewelry they stock is often displayed purely as accessories for clothes. They might well throw a rare 1930s Eisenberg in with a bundle of indifferent 1960s junk; the collector's job is to recognize the difference. Good costume pieces can also turn up at thrift stores, garage sales, junk stores, and dress agencies.

Fakes and Forgeries

Because period costume jewelry has become enormously popular over the last decade, prices have risen sharply. The downside has been the inevitable appearance of fakes and forgeries. This applies in particular to Art Deco jewelry, Trifari "jelly-belly" animals, early Eisenbergs, Schiaparellis, and Corocraft pieces. A forgery is likely to bear exactly the same maker's mark as an original, and may have been deliberately aged to deceive the untrained eye. Good costume jewelry is still difficult and expensive to make, so forgeries tend to appear only at the pricey end of the market. The mid and lower price ranges are therefore fairly safe territory for the novice collector who might be shopping in street fairs or markets. Most forgeries appear at this kind of sale, on the stalls of nonspecialist dealers who have themselves been taken in and are now, unwittingly, selling them on to the public. It would be wrong to avoid fairs and markets altogether, as they are fun, economical, and rich sources of costume jewelry, but it would be wise to confine your purchases there to inexpensive pieces until you are confident that you can spot a fake.

Legitimate Reproduction

The collector must also be aware of perfectly legitimate reproductions. Firms like Butler and Wilson make a point of copying a wide range of earlier styles, and the Miriam Haskell company, still very much a going concern, has reissued some of its own 1940s and 50s designs to cash in on the fashionability of period costume jewelry. Unlike forgeries, these are not produced with any intention to deceive, but some of them nevertheless find their way into the antiques trade.

The collector's best defense against these confusing pitfalls is the same as for any kind of antique. Before you buy, take the time to learn the facts and educate your eye. Reference books are the best starting point, but they are no substitute for actually looking at jewelry. Visit specialist stores, handle the jewelry, weigh it in your hand, examine it closely, and ask lots of questions. Most dealers have chosen to specialize because they love costume jewelry and want to share their enthusiasm. Dealers know that anyone whose interest in the subject is deeper than a simple admiration is a collector in the making, and collectors are the lifeblood of their business. A reputable, established dealer will be happy to give you historical information and practical tips, in the knowledge that your aim, at that point, is to learn rather than to buy.

Caring for Fragile Pieces

By all means wear your costume jewelry, as this is one of the chief pleasures of owning it, but do keep in mind that pieces may be fragile, and need careful handling. Always apply hairspray, soap, cream, or perfume before you put on jewelry, as cosmetics can damage plated surfaces, faux pearls, jet, and beads. Before wearing, check that chain links, settings, and clasps are secure, as these can weaken over time. Never immerse costume jewelry in water, as this

Careful scrutiny will show that these are not genuine Schiaparelli earrings but shrewd fakes that play on a subtle misspelling of her name. Steinberg & Tolkien, London.

If a stone is lost (above), modern clear pastes are readily available, along with straightforward colors. Frosted stones and more unusual shades like fuschia, olive green, and orange are harder to come by. Steinberg & Tolkien, London.

This kind of junk box (left) is common at fleamarkets and fairs, and it is always worth rummaging through for hidden treasure.

Unusual colors present restoration problems, but unusual textures can be a nightmare. These kinds of stones (*above*) are not much made today, so it is vital to build up a stock of period pastes. Specialist dealers can also help with difficult repairs. Steinberg & Tolkien, London.

Double-pronged, fur-clip bearing the Trifari signature (*top*); flat-backed dress-clip, unsigned. Marc Steinberg, St. Louis.

can dissolve adhesive, tarnish metal, discolor paste, and shrink or rot string on beaded necklaces and bracelets. However, if a beaded piece does break, insist that it is restrung on string as opposed to clear nylon or wire; while these are stronger, they quickly stretch or bend out of shape. To clean paste stones spray a cotton bud with a small amount of window cleaning liquid, squeeze the bud to remove the excess then gently buff only the surface of each stone. Make sure that the cleaner does not seep into any settings. Pat dry with a cotton cloth. To revitalize tired-looking metal settings, use a jeweler's cloth, available from specialist dealers and some hardware or department stores. Avoid polishing creams or dips, and try not to over-polish, as patina is desirable on all but the shiniest rhodium finishes, and these rarely tarnish anyway. Store each piece individually in its own box or cloth pochette if possible, but if not, wrap it in acid-free paper, which is available from many antique dealers.

Repair and Refurbishment
The biggest problem with stone-set jewelry is the inevitable loss of paste stones. Proper storage and common sense will minimize the risk, but some paste loss is inevitable. Your favorite dealer will usually be able to arrange repairs, but they can be costly, and often you have to part with your piece for several weeks, as good repair services are generally overstretched, and turn-around correspondingly slow.

It is perfectly possible and legitimate to replace your own pastes, and many collectors maintain a supply of both old and new stones for this purpose. Some gem and lapidary wholesalers, as well as art, craft, and hobby stores, stock pastes, marcasites, and faux pearls, and your dealer should be able to put you in touch with the best local sources for these.

It is always worth buying broken bits of jewelry offered for a pittance at fleamarkets and garage sales, particularly if they have unusual pastes, cabochons, beads, clasps, or pearls. While clear (white) rhinestones and standard colors are still produced and widely available, some of the textured, "aurora," or other unusual stones are not. New faux pearls rarely match the tones of period ones, and an antique necklace can be seriously let down by a brand new, shiny-looking replacement clasp.

To replace lost stones it is best to use clear-drying jeweler's cement, which can be bought through dealers or craft and hobby shops, but if none is available any of the super-strong adhesives that bond glass to metal will work. To replace stones, apply a tiny dewdrop of your chosen adhesive on to the end of a safety pin and dab this into the cup-like setting, taking care not to fill it to the edge or the adhesive will spill over. If you see that you have applied too much, a twisted corner of tissue can be used as a wick to absorb excess. A clean cotton cloth should also be kept standing by for major spills. Never let excess adhesive dry on a stone or setting, as it will be difficult to remove later. Next, pick up your stone, either with your fingers or with tweezers, and push it gently into the setting, then leave it to dry for at least two hours. With prongset pieces, the prongs have to be carefully opened with a pair of slim-nosed jeweler's pliers prior to paste replacement, and reclosed after the adhesive has dried.

For anything more complex than a lost stone or two, repairs should be carried out by a skilled person. Many precious jewelers refuse to repair costume jewelry; although some jewelers may undertake repairs, they may not possess the skill, since the metals involved are often very different from those they are used to working with. Bead restringing is usually done well by traditional jewelry repairers, but for anything that involves soldering it is best to find a specialist through one of your local costume jewelry dealers.

If a stone is missing or a snakechain is snapped, repairs must be carried out, but the subject of restoration is one upon which collectors are divided. Many of those who wear their jewelry want it to look pristine, and therefore think nothing of replating or re-enameling settings or replacing all the stones in a tired-looking piece with brand new pastes. Other collectors would never under any circumstances buy a piece that has undergone this type of restoration. Because costume jewelry is one of the few usable antiques, and should be bought for pleasure rather than investment, the question of whether or not to restore must ultimately come down to the wearer's preference. If a dull finish or discolored stones spoil your pleasure in a piece that you otherwise love to wear, then by all means buy, restore, and enjoy it.

Dating and Signatures

Precise dating of costume jewelry is usually impossible. The best that can be hoped for is an educated guess based on style and materials. You can certainly develop a feel for the characteristics of the various eras by examining pieces and studying books; in the case of 20th-century styles, old fashion magazines, often kept in library reference archives, can prove invaluable. Even the American cocktail jewelry which was mass-produced by large companies is difficult to pinpoint as the patent numbers which the pieces sometimes bear give only a rough idea of a date. A particular design, for example, may not have been patented until proven popular; it may then have been repeated over several decades, or the patent may in fact refer to a clip-back or some other technical innovation which has nothing to do with the design at all.

While most of the earliest costume jewelry is unsigned, by the late 19th century more pieces bore a manufacturer's or designer's mark. As a very rough guide, American jewelry usually bears a full signature, while European pieces tend to be marked with initials, symbols, or hallmarks. The most important American exceptions to this rule are worth learning, as they are so few. The early mark for Trifari is "KTF," Eisenberg may be signed "E," Hattie Carnegie sometimes appears as "H.C.," early Ken Lane is signed "K.J.L.," and early Boucher bears a stylized bird's-head mark. Otherwise, a signed Miriam Haskell will say "Haskell," a later Trifari will be marked "Trifari," and so on.

Marks can appear on clasps, earring backs, brooch backs, or the inside of catches. Sometimes a mark is stamped so minutely on a tiny jump ring closure that it takes a jeweler's loupe to see it.

While much American jewelry was signed by the mid-1930s, confusingly a great deal was not. Many of the best pieces are in fact unsigned, which should not deter the buyer provided the piece is interesting and attractive. A designer's name cannot compensate for a boring design, poor quality or condition. Many companies produced jewelry at all price levels, but only top-of-the-line pieces command the best prices today. It is a common mistake among novice dealers and collectors to think that the name "Trifari" or "Coro" automatically makes a piece worthwhile. Ironically, some of the most mediocre designs were originally produced in vast quantities over long periods, as their very insipidity meant that they blended into every era and offended no one.

Most costume jewelry is anonymous, but a piece, particularly from the 20th century, might be prominently signed by a designer or manufacturer. Or it might bear only the tiniest, most unobtrusive hallmark on a clasp or jump ring. Steinberg & Tolkien, London.

These 1940s, 50s and 60s cufflinks by American firms like Swank are still sold very cheaply in markets, but many were made to the same standard as women's costume jewelry. Some collectors buy shirts with buttonless cuffs so they can show off this undiscovered area of costume jewelry. Steinberg & Tolkien, London.

INFLUENCES AND INSPIRATIONS

Long before the first cities were built, or the first nuggets of gold were turned into coveted jewels, humans were transforming the natural objects they found into decorative artifacts to wear. The urge for self-adornment has resulted in a legacy of jewelry that stretches back thousands of years, much of it made from precious materials, but far more fashioned from everyday organic matter, for sheer visual pleasure.

Since early times, man has created adornment in imitation of nature. Floral motifs, such as these used by costume jewelry designer Stanley Hagler in the 1960s, are as old as jewelry itself. Steven Miners, Cristobal, London.

The earliest pieces of jewelry may well have played a dual role, as both decoration and as an amulet, to ward off evil spirits, but there is no doubt that humans had a particular interest in enhancing their own bodies and in imitating the beauty of natural forms. To this day, jewelry is fashioned into shapes and designs drawn directly from nature: a colorful flower, a quivering feather, the profile of a woman's face. Flower motifs and the female face were favorites of Art Nouveau jewelers.

Over the centuries, such motifs have appeared again and again in countless different and often unconnected cultures, each portraying the themes of nature in their individual ways. Such homage to the natural world is hardly surprising, given that it also provided all the jeweler might need to fulfill his craft. An endless array of suitable materials to mold and polish was on hand, in an extraordinary range of colors, shapes, and textures. Shells, fish, and animal bones were transformed into rings, pendants, and necklaces by the earliest men and women, while the tusks, horns, and teeth of mammoths, walruses, and reindeer were being carved as part of a thriving ivory trade over 30,000 years ago. Clay, stone, and natural glass such as obsidian were obvious candidates for beads. The Barbaric style of the 1920s and 30s, an offshoot of Art Deco, is a reflection of these early, "primitive" artifacts, and glass beads have been used in every modern style of jewelry, either to imitate precious stones or as attractive jewels in their own right.

Gold's potential as a decorative metal is first thought to have been realized in Mesopotamia (present-day Iraq) around 3000 B.C., and it quickly became established as the most highly sought metals. Its natural properties, a rich, gleaming color which never faded, and its malleability, which allowed it to be easily worked with the rudimentary tools of the time, made it a jeweler's dream. The metal was endlessly crafted into beautiful forms, reflecting the cultures that created them, cultures as diverse as those of the Sumerians in Mesopotamia, the Egyptians, the Etruscans in northern Italy, the Celts of northern Europe, and the indigenous peoples of South America and Africa.

The Sharing of Skills

The contemporary cultures of North Africa, Europe, and the Near and Middle East including Asia Minor, were already linked through well-established trade routes by the time of the Sumerians, around 3000 B.C.

These modern pieces from Fior reflect the influences of ancient Mediterranean culture on contemporary jewelry design. Fior, London.

Indeed, the Sumerians, who were considered consummate jewelers, actually imported their most precious materials, gold, silver, and semiprecious stones such as lapis lazuli. They had already mastered many of the jewelry techniques still used today, such as granulation (where small dots of gold or other materials are soldered onto a base), and filigree work, where fine gold wire was bent into decorative shapes, designed to be left as openwork, applied to a solid base, or to hold precious stones or enamel.

The advances of the Sumerians were absorbed by the ancient Egyptians, who developed a very distinctive style of jewelry, out of step with that of their neighbors. The Egyptians were unique in making jewelry as a clear means of representation, ignoring purely decorative techniques such as filigree in favor of clearly defined, graphic designs that mirrored their pictorial hieroglyphic writing.

The people of ancient Egypt were conservative; it took them a thousand years or so longer than neighboring cultures to adopt the habit of wearing earrings. Their distinctive designs, however, proved popular and enduring, revived time and again by the jewelers of later societies. An explosion of interest was created during the Art Deco period of the 1920s, when the opening of sealed Egyptian tombs had a profound impact on all the decorative arts, including jewelry design.

The Egyptian style was absorbed and expanded by the Phoenicians, whose trading empire spread out around 1200 B.C. from the coastal regions of Syria and Lebanon to North Africa, Cyprus, and across the Mediterranean to Spain. The Phoenicians, too, were expert jewelers. Their techniques were later replicated in the superb jewelry of the Etruscans, who inhabited what is now the Tuscan and Umbrian regions of present-day Italy around 500 B.C.

Part of a 1960s bracelet and earrings set by Kenneth Jay Lane; the ram's head earrings owe much to ancient jewelry design. Marc Steinberg, St. Louis.

A fascination with all things Egyptian inspired many famous jewelers. This 1920s bracelet of diamonds, emeralds, rubies, sapphires, and onyx set in platinium by Van Cleef & Arpels is a fine example of Egyptomania. Van Cleef & Arpels, Paris

Again, the discovery of previously undisturbed hoards of delicate Etruscan jewelry near Rome in the mid-19th century provoked a vogue for "archeological" jewelry, which continued its influence well into the 20th century. Farther north, the Celts of the same period were fascinated by gold. They fashioned it into torques and bracelets using the most basic of metal, wood, or bone tools, decorating the surfaces with distinctive floral and animal motifs that seem amazingly contemporary. They are familiar to us through the late 19th-century British Arts and Crafts movement, which sparked a Celtic revival through the creations of the well-known London firm, Liberty & Co. Celtic jewelry went on to influence that of the Vikings, the Anglo-Saxons, and other cultures of northern Europe, although these came to be dominated by the spread of the most powerful contemporary culture, that of the Romans.

By the time the Hellenistic culture of ancient Greece held sway in the Middle and Near East, around 350 B.C., there was an almost complete uniformity in jewelry design in the region. Intricate filigree work was made into flower sprays, spirals, and waves, and often filled with enamel, while garnets, onyxes, emeralds, and pearls were most frequently selected. Before long, however, the Roman taste was in the ascendant, although it absorbed many aspects of the Greek style, including the liking for emeralds, pearls, and sapphires.

Much Roman jewelry abandoned complicated filigree in favor of starker, smoother planes of burnished gold. As Christianity took hold throughout the Empire, Christian motifs appeared. Sometimes these were, in fact, much older images, and many of them have continued to be reworked up till today. The lotus flower became a symbol for the Virgin Mary, and the birth of Christ, for example, but it was also a recognized motif in ancient Egyptian jewelry, as it was believed that the sun god, Horus, was born in a lotus flower.

Design to Meet Supply

By the time the Roman civilization was in decline in the 4th century A.D., a wealth of natural resources was available to jewelers working in Europe, North Africa, and the Middle East. The pearls so prized by the Romans were readily available from the coasts of northern India and the Red Sea; emeralds were discovered in Egypt; gold was being mined in Sudan, Egypt, Syria, Turkey, Greece, Italy, France, Portugal, Ireland, and England. Amber was found in Britain and Poland, ivory in Ethiopia and India, lapis lazuli in Afghanistan, and garnets, cornelian, and onyx on the Indian continent.

Every different material inspired a new approach to design and technique. The human predilection for experiment soon led to the manufacture of a number of manmade materials for jewelry, the first of which, glass, was in full-scale production by 3000 B.C., around the time that gold was discovered. From the earliest days right up to the present, glass was used to make cheaper versions of expensive jewels, some of which were clear imitations, others deliberate fakes.

Over the centuries, glassmaking became increasingly refined, at first cast, then pulled, into a wide range of imitation gemstones. By the early 17th century, glass gems of the highest quality were emerging from the manufacturing centers of Venice and Bohemia, and these stones encouraged jewelers to experiment further with designs and settings, especially after the introduction of machine cutting, when large quantities of glass stones of regular size and matching quality could be turned out.

Alchemists were hard at work finding alternatives to gold, inventing a variety of metal alloys and gilt metals to use in its place. Silver came into its own with the rise of the diamond and its colorless glass imitation, known as paste, while cut steel, a hard, durable alloy of iron and carbon long used for swords and other implements, became a fashionable alternative, though not a

This gilt metal brooch, *c*. mid 17th century, by Roman art jeweler Fortunato Pio Castellani, reflects his great love of ancient Greek and Etruscan styles. Beauty & the Beasts, London.

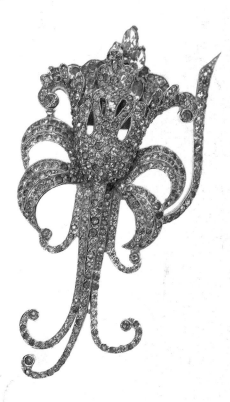

A great deal of paste was created to imitate the sparkle of real diamonds. This Coro 1930s brooch of white pastes is set in rhodium. Steinberg & Tolkien, London.

Egyptian revival suite of silver, enamel, carved chalcedony, cornelian, and turquoise, *c*. 1910 (*opposite page*) is a German Art Nouveau interpretation of an ancient style. Tadema Gallery, London.

Cosmetic queen Helena Rubenstein, who launched salons in Paris and London at the beginning of the 20th century, helped create the modern cosmetics industry which flourished along side that of costume jewelry.

substitute, for diamonds in the 18th century. The experience of working with inexpensive materials such as these was invaluable, particularly for 20th-century jewelers, who incorporated all of these materials in pieces produced during the heyday of costume jewelry. But by far the most revolutionary of the modern materials to be invented, and the most influential on the development of true costume jewelry, were the plastics. The earliest plastics were discovered in the mid-19th century, and were made from cellulose, the natural fiber of plants. The discovery by scientists that cellulose could be extracted and then reconstituted into a substance that was malleable when liquid but hard once set was a breakthrough, with far-reaching implications for jewelry production, and society, that were unimaginable at the time.

Jewelry to Match the Times

The creative uses of plastics were endless. Before long, they were used to imitate various types of organic matter, from coral to tortoiseshell. It was another 70 years or so before plastics were appreciated as materials in their own right, however, and as so often with major shifts in design or taste, it was a combination of different social factors that made plastics such as Bakelite significant in the jewelry of the Art Deco period and subsequent years.

The public adulation of well-known figures, such as the actress Sarah Bernhardt, who rose to fame in the 1890s, was fueled by the rise of the American film industry and its stars. The related cosmetics industry was already flourishing by the time that the American Elizabeth Arden and her rival, the Austrian Helena Rubenstein, launched beauty salons in Paris and London in 1908. This was also the year that Max Factor, a Russian who had worked for the Czar as a cosmetician, arrived in Hollywood.

Max Factor revolutionized film make-up, introducing the term itself in 1920, and, in the process, greatly influenced millions of women around the globe who idolized the stars of the silver screen. These women slavishly followed every aspect of the Hollywood icons, imitating their behavior, make-up, dress, hair, and, of course, their jewelry.

This love affair with Hollywood coincided with another social upheaval in the United States: the Depression years. As wealthy Americans watched their comfortable lifestyle evaporate from 1929 on, and the living conditions of those with little money became ever more desperate, the costume jewelry industry, based in Providence, Rhode Island, reaped the benefits. Only a very

The Whitby jet necklace, brooch, and bracelets show how the medium lent itself to both high relief and delicate intaglio carving, as well as simple designs which displayed its high polish.

New materials, such as ivorine and Bakelite, had a profound effect on costume jewelry design. This hair comb was an early product of mass production. Trevor Allen, London.

few could afford precious jewelry, and even then they were loath to be seen wearing it, preferring to adorn themselves with more socially acceptable costume pieces at a time of general suffering.

When Hitler came to power in Germany in 1933, heralding disaster in Europe, the American costume jewelry trade was well placed to welcome the flood of refugees that poured steadily in. From the early 1930s and well into the 1940s, Providence provided work for hundreds of experienced European craftsmen, jewelers, and goldsmiths fleeing the rise of Fascism and the persecution of Jewish minorities. They brought with them the experience of generations in working with precious gems and metals, and were able to turn these skills to good use, producing wonderful costume jewelry. So fine was their work that they guaranteed the continuing patronage of even the wealthy once life returned to normal.

This mass movement of skilled craftsmen, forced by circumstance to adapt their skills to downscale materials, had remarkable echoes of earlier times. A similar exodus had taken place during the late 17th century from France to England, when Huguenot silversmiths fled to avoid persecution by Catholics, taking with them their experience of precious metal-working. During the French Revolution at the end of the 18th century, the trade in precious jewelry all but ceased, forcing goldsmiths to work with cheaper materials befitting the social attitudes of the time.

In both these earlier periods, enforced changes created a moment ripe for a radical shift in design. Sometimes jewelers found themselves freed from conventions that had been in place for decades and could indulge their imaginations to the full. A similar dynamic was at work in 1920s America, where intellectuals and designers newly arrived from Austria and Germany were able to explore and extend, in cheap materials such as plastic and glass, the revolutionary geometric ideas of the Wiener Werkstätte and the Bauhaus, two of the most influential artistic movements in Europe during the early part of the 20th century.

Inextricably linked to the rise of both the film industry and the related fashion and couture trades, the result of this convergence was a profusion of colorful, witty, affordable jewels that continued to be popular with rich and poor alike. The age of the 20th-century costume jewel was launched, bringing excitement and color to women around the world.

This early 1920s enamel, chrome, and Bakelite bracelet from Germany reflects the European fashion for mixing Bakelite with other materials. Christopher St. James, Ritzy, London.

CHAPTER ONE

Aristocratic Adornment

Fashionable men and women of the 18th century decked themselves out in powder, eye patches, beauty spots, and fine costumes. Sparkling jewels provided the finishing touches. Beeswax candles, newly invented and giving a brighter light than tallow, reflected off mirrors, chandeliers, and diamonds to provide the nighttime glitter that this age of prosperity enjoyed so much. The demand for sparkle could not be met with existing precious gems, so the development of paste in the form of fake diamonds and other precious gems met with widespread acceptance.

THE AGE OF ARTIFICE

The development of paste in the 18th century revolutionized the jewelry trade in Europe, and allowed jewelers the freedom to experiment with cutting and shaping in ways that were unimaginable with precious stones.

The 18th century in Europe was for many an affluent and exciting time. London made the most of its position as the world's leading port, processing newly discovered treasures from the Americas and the Far East, while Paris glittered with the extravagances of the courts of Louis XV (reigned 1715–74) and his son, Louis XVI (reigned 1774–92). It was a century of great contrasts, with hopeless poverty the lot of the lower classes, while the traditionally rich aristocrats were joined increasingly by a rising middle class, who made their fortunes through banking, artistic merit, trading, politics, or corruption. They enjoyed their wealth in a continual sweep of balls, dinners, private race meetings, and gambling evenings, relaxing during the day in elegant rooms and private libraries. While education and intellectual inquiry were considered highly desirable, spending money was a favorite pastime; fortunes were won and lost at the gaming tables and bankruptcy was no shame, as long as it was achieved with style. A passion for large set jewels had been inherited in both France and Britain from the previous century. Above all, diamonds were prized for their flashing, icy fire, for their flattering ability to frame a fashionable face and draw attention to a handsome bust. The breasts were pushed up by low-cut bodices, revealing an expanse of bosom that cried out for jewels, while earrings dangled almost to shoulder level from ears exposed by hair swept up and back. Diamond jewels came into their own particularly at night, reflecting candlelight from the faceted stones onto the features of

The white and colored paste cluster brooches (*top left*) *c.* 1785, were originally buttons. The pink paste border is unusual and increases the value of the piece. The shape of the girandole pendant earrings of rock crystal (*top right*) *c.* 1760, is typical of the period. White paste shoe buckles (*bottom left*) *c.* 1790, would have been worn by both men and women. Harvey & Gore, London. This exquisite brooch (*bottom right*) *c.* 1725, alternates clear and opaline pastes around a magnificent opaline paste center. Beauty & the Beasts, London.

Marie Antoinette, wife of the French King Louis XVI, was notorious for her extravagance. She popularized the fashion for towering dressed hair. She lost her head to the guillotine during the French Revolution as a result of her excesses.

the wearer. Men and women at courts all over Europe, like generations before them, used sparkling gemstones set in gold as a means of displaying their status and wealth, setting them in buttons, buckles, brooches, hair ornaments, sword hilts, watches, corsages, earrings, and necklaces.

As a greater distinction grew up between day and nighttime activities and entertainments, so too did a divide appear between evening and daytime clothes, known as "dress" and "undress," and the items of jewelry to accompany them. Then as now, daytime jewels were quieter and more restrained than the glittering items worn in the evening.

Court Fashions Set the Trends

Early in the century, appearance was everything, and the expanding middle classes slavishly followed the prevailing court fashions of the day, keen to appear in touch with the highest ranking socialites. This accounted for the eagerness to embrace some of the more impractical or even ridiculous fashions. In addition to painting the face white with lead and mercury, despite the known risks, women also saddled themselves with immense, uncomfortable hairstyles that were both unhygienic and inconvenient. Towering edifices of real and false hair were held in place with wire, padding, and pomade, before being powdered and decorated with feathers, bows, flowers, and jewels of all kinds. Pride in their fashionable appearance forced many women to travel with their heads outside the carriage, as their hairpieces were too tall to fit inside.

This style, which was to reach its most absurd extreme late in the century at the French court of Louis XVI, epitomizing the spoiled preoccupations and fancies of his queen, Marie Antoinette, gave rise to the most popular jewel of the time, the pompon. A large hair ornament of velvet, feathers, ribbons, and imitation gems, the pompon was designed specifically to decorate these elaborate hair arrangements, and in the mid-18th century was the modish equivalent of the *aigrette*, an ornament traceable back to medieval Europe, Persia, and Mughal India. Originally the *aigrette* was a hair or hat ornament that held real or jeweled feathers, although by the 18th century it often took the form of a flower bouquet or crescent spray.

The Development of Paste Jewels

Few members of the expanding class of gentry could afford diamonds, which were relatively rare and therefore valuable. The stones, rather than their settings, were the important element in early 18th-century jewels, so there was a pressing need to find a way to make successful substitutes for both colored gemstones and diamonds. A solution was found in northern Bohemia (in the present-day Czech Republic), a region rich in precious and semi-precious minerals such as agate, cornelian, jasper, and sapphire, which also had an abundance of wood, quartz, and water, the basic natural resources needed to produce glass. As early as the late 16th century, the town of Gablonz (now Jablonec), in the center of the region, had developed a reputation for its superb cutting of gemstones, and these skills stood its gemcutters in good stead when they realized that they could imitate the precious stones in glass. By 1709, high-quality imitation stones made from glass composition (a type of glass with a high lead content) were already being imported into Venice from Bohemia. Most of these paste "stones" were made by casting the glass in clay molds, but by 1750 the techniques had changed; the glass was now drawn out with long rods and then cut into sections. By 1761, the Gablonz firm of Jan Frantisek Schwan had supplied nearly 250,000 "garnets" to Piacenza in Italy, as well as exporting colored glass stones to Germany and further afield.

Enhancing Color

A thriving costume jewelry business was developing in Europe, based on a remarkable selection of colored glass stones, which flattered the wearer in the same way as true stones and gave an impression of luxurious wealth without costing a fortune. Foiling the stones was done to increase their fire and depth of color. Traditionally, gemstones were backed with paper-thin sheets of bright metal, often silver or copper. Some of these foils were tinted. As the foils tended to erode and mark when they were exposed to air, the mounts for the stones had to be airtight; the jeweler pinched them tightly, so that there was no possibility of air getting to the foil lining.

Foiling was used on all stones of the period, and some of the workmanship involved in setting good 18th-century pastes was finer than that on more expensive jewelry. This was because it was often easier to foil precious stones

Floral jewels were eternally popular, especially during the late 18th century. Many employed colored pastes, as seen in this brooch, c. 1790. Harvey & Gore, London.

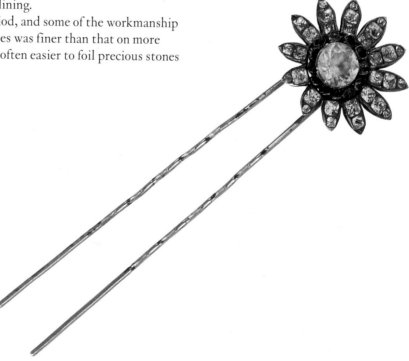

Yellow and amethyst paste flower, c. 1770, attached to a later hair mounting. Such hair pins were extensively used to draw attention to extravagant hair arrangements popularized by Marie Antoinette. Harvey & Gore, London.

than pastes, as the genuine article tended to be more durable. On good-quality 18th-century paste, there is rarely any hint of the foil behind the stone, which was sealed in place in smooth-backed cups of metal, gold for colored pastes, or silver for imitation diamonds. Later examples are sometimes identifiable by inexpert foiling which has crumpled or changed color with time.

Discoloration can also be caused by damp. It is very important to keep paste of any date in a dry environment and not to clean it by washing. Once the stones and foils become wet, they will inevitably discolor.

The Freedom of Working with Paste

Although originally intended for copies of precious jewelry, the plentiful supply of colored or colorless "gems" arriving in jewelers' workshops from the earliest years of the century allowed a freedom of artistic creativity previously unimagined. For the first time, they could experiment, cutting and shaping the paste in ways that earlier, genuine stones were too expensive to allow. This also meant that the jewelry was appreciated for its artistic merit, over and above its intrinsic worth. But while these glass stones from Bohemia were wonderful for costume and daytime jewels, they were not generally of a high enough standard to be a convincing alternative to diamonds. Since the brilliant cut for the diamond (a way of cutting the stone into 58 facets to release its maximum fire that was generally credited to the Venetian cardinal Vincenzo Peruzzi,) had been discovered in the late 17th century, glassmakers and jewelers alike had looked for a substitute that could be treated in the same way. The glass that emerged from Venice and Bohemia was simply not hard enough. One source of substitute stones was rock crystal, a naturally occurring colorless quartz from which brilliants were commonly cut. To increase the brilliance, the stones were faceted and foil-backed before being set, and were often incorporated into men's buttons and buckles. The crystals were widely found and frequently worn in Spain and Portugal. A seam near Bristol provided the English market with an ample supply, sometimes known as Bristows or Bristol stones, and the Rhine and Alençon areas of France supplied crystal stones to the jewelers of Paris.

A Glass that Sparkled like Diamonds

A glass that was suitable for treatment like a diamond had been invented in England in the mid-17th century by George Ravenscroft (1618–81), a technician with the Glass Sellers Company of London. Until 1660 or so, the company had made a glass based on a highly secret Venetian formula (imported by refugees settling in London), which required the addition of a powder made from Venetian pebbles. Ravenscroft decided to investigate the possibility of making an entirely English glass and substituted English flint for the pebbles. When he also changed the potash in the formula to soda, around 1675–6, he succeeded in creating a crack-free English lead glass, which became renowned for its fine quality. Although the lead content made it slightly softer than ordinary glass, it created a material that sparkled more brightly and refracted color better. This quality made Ravenscroft's glass ideally suited to the purpose; it was still hard enough to withstand the stresses of cutting, polishing, and setting. His invention did not affect the jewelry world until the Frenchman Georges Frèdèric Stras, born in the earliest years of the 18th century, realized the potential of English lead glass and explored its possibilities as a diamond substitute.

It was Stras above all others who was responsible for establishing paste jewels as more than simply imitation diamonds, but as remarkable creations acceptable in their own right. For the first time, jewelers could choose from a massive range of precious and nonprecious materials to work with, and the opportunities for creating highly imaginative jewels were vast. They now had

Paste was always backed by an extremely thin layer of foil, but this can become discolored with time because of damp or exposure to air, as seen on parts of this lyre brooch, *c.* 1800. Harvey & Gore, London.

the freedom to explore different cuts for the stones, and this in turn led to new ideas about how to set and present them. The design of a jewel became significant as jewelers vied to show off the stones at their best, butting them together so that the mounts were barely visible. Immense skill was involved in working out what setting brought out the best in the stones, and what metals best suited the colors of stone available. Many eye-catching pieces typical of the 18th century, were laden with big and small stones. They often reflected the passion for flowers and nature fostered originally by the florid baroque style of 17th-century Europe. By the time the frivolous and elaborate rococo style came to dominate in the mid-1740s, fashionable jewels were incorporating simplistic, stylized interpretations of natural phenomena, from flowers to insects and butterflies.

Most of the 18th-century paste that comes up for sale today is made with colorless, rather than colored, stones. The early colored paste pieces are very

Shoe Buckles

■ From the mid-17th century on, shoes were decorated with paste buckles in order to draw attention to the nimble-footed dancer. By the 1740s, the footwear of most courtiers in France and England glittered and shone. High fashion demanded that both men and women of substance sparkled from head to toe, and buckles, often festooned with jewels, were used to decorate hats and breeches as well as shoes. During the great paste era of the 1740s and 1750s, shoe buckles were considered more than mere adjuncts to fashion: it was said that you could tell a man's social standing by the elegance and extravagance of his buckles. Those who considered themselves the last word in fashion sported the most outrageous buckles, sometimes extending down the sides of the shoes; the pair of yellow and white paste men's buckles c.1790 (*above right*, Harvey & Gore, London) shows the fashion taken to its extreme.

Paste buckles were made in quantity in the late 18th century by firms such as Matthew Boulton of Birmingham. However, toward the end of the century, the invention of the shoelace changed the design of shoes and rendered the buckle redundant. Buckles are a good idea for a new collector, as they are still found in considerable numbers and sell for very reasonable sums. Most date from the late 18th and early 19th centuries, and are usually decorated with colorless paste, although some of the most highly sought are set with Bristol blue glass, and are accordingly expensive.

As with other types of jewelry, buckles found with their original silk-lined cases are worth considerably more than those without, as cases of that age are rare and unusual. One disadvantage of collecting buckles is that they have little practical use today, although some have been converted into brooches. This is a shame, however, as their original fittings are lost in the process.

The Ultimate in Fake Diamonds

■ Georges Frédéric Stras (1701–73) became rich and famous through his extraordinary talent as a gemcutter and setter. His work with colorless glass paste jewelry was so well known that it was named for him, and is still known as "strass" in some circles to this day. Stras, who was born in Wolfisheim, near Strasbourg, in France, first learned his trade when he worked as an apprentice between the ages of 13 and 18 with a Strasbourg goldsmith, Abraham Spach. In 1724, at just 23, he moved to Paris and joined a small but fashionable jewelry business there. Before long, his work attracted the notice of others in the small, exclusive circle of high-class Parisian jewelers, and he started to experiment with setting the fine glass stones that were available in quantity from England and Bohemia. Within a few years, he had made his name cutting and setting paste into spectacular, albeit imitation, jewelry, marked with his initials, GFS, and a crowned sword.

By 1734, when he was appointed official jeweler to the King of France, his pieces were being worn by those of most ranks in society, including the most aristocratic. Madame du Barry, a favorite of Louis XV, owned a pair of his blue earrings, giving the seal of court approval to paste jewels.

Some time around 1750, a German goldsmith working in Paris, Georges Michel Bapst, joined the business, taking over just two years later, before marrying Stras's niece in 1755. As Stras became more established in his career, he worked less and less with paste, preferring to use real diamonds, but the two worked together at Stras's shop in the Quai des Orfévres until his death, and the business continued to provide jewels for the rich and well-known, such as Madame de Pompadour, another of the king's mistresses. The Bapst family went on to produce some of the most illustrious of French crown jewelers, and was still renowned in the 19th century as the firm Bapst et Falize.

Many late 18th-century English pendants and brooches were executed in the shape of a Maltese cross. This particular example is set with white paste stones. Trevor Allen, London.

unusual, and even a small pansy brooch or daisy-head barrette in good condition can sell for a considerable sum. Even though there was far more colorless paste made at the time, good examples in fine condition are relatively hard to come by. A *riviére* necklace (literally a river of stones) from the late 18th century will go for a high price at an auction sale, considerably more through private dealers. Many early paste buttons were converted into cufflinks, attached to each other with a short length of chain, while some of the larger buttons were made into brooches.

Male Adornment

Men were as interested in fashion as women, and just as likely to spend extravagantly on fashion accessories, from mouse-skin face patches to wigs. Indeed, wigs were so expensive that one inventive wigmaker boasted "a wig of copper wire which resists all weathers and will last forever" in an advertisement of 1750.

Men were equally drawn to jewels. Sets of matching buttons were considered essential; some might be set with paste or real gems, while others were ornamented with enamelwork. Many of these buttons were purely decorative, rather than functional. Some were decorated with illustrations of sporting pursuits, others served as commemoration of a well-known battle. From the 1770s on, clothes became less flamboyant, but buttons, conversely, became larger and more decorative.

Jewels on the Move

By the 1750s, various echelons of society were to be seen wearing paste jewels set on steel springs, allowing them to "tremble" as their wearers moved. This device was particularly favored for the pompon, as well as for brooches and corsage sprays. Patrons in London bought their paste at such fashionable shops as Wickes & Netherton, a renowned establishment patronized by the aristocratic and wealthy, and which sold top-quality paste pieces alongside the most precious of jewels. The shop was first set up in 1722 by George Wickes, and in 1802 came to be known as Garrards.

In France, fashionable men and women would meet on shopping expeditions for the latest jewels in the Paris outlets of makers such as Stras, Bapst, Chèron, and Lancon, all of whom were renowned for their skilled cutting and setting of glass stones. Indeed, working with paste had become such a successful trade in Paris that, by the 1760s, over 300 skillful jewelers and admired designers were working within the guild of *bijoutiers-faussetiers*, or false jewelers.

To balance the towering hairstyles that so dominated women's fashion at this time, earrings played an important part for evening or formal wear. Most were long, with a drop of up to 2 inches (5cm), and some were simple, single-drop designs. Others were more complex and sophisticated, such as the girandole earrings, whixch were chandelier-shaped pieces with a large central stone surrounded by smaller ones and typical of the period. These were often made in France, where fashions tended to be bolder and more flamboyant than in England.

The Emergence of Matching Sets

Parures, matching sets of jewelry, first emerged during the early years of the 18th century and evolved out of the late 17th-century fad for elegantly matching buttons, aigrettes, and similar accessories. They almost always included a pair of earrings, a necklace, a brooch, and bracelets. Some sets also included hair ornaments and combs.

Depending on their wealth and status, women would own several sets of such jewels in different colors of gems or paste, some of which would be suitable for evening wear, others in gentle colors for daytime use. Demi-parures were also commonplace, combining a pair of earrings with a necklace, a brooch, or an aigrette. Parures that are still in their cases are up to twice as valuable as those without, both because the cases, like the jewels they contained, tended to be large, flamboyant, and exhibitionist, and also because surviving sets in good condition from the late 18th century are rare.

There are slightly more examples from the early 19th century. One set, of amethysts and gold, still with its case, was taken out of France by an aristocrat fleeing the Revolution and given to an English family in payment for their help. The parure remained in the family from that date, and was sold in the mid-1990s, fetching a very handsome price at auction.

Pompons and Bows

Jewelers worked hard to imitate in paste jewelry the fall of fabric, creating bows from loops of finely worked silver that shimmered with faceted stones. Such luxurious bows came to be known as Sévignés, named after Madame de Sévigné, a well-known Parisian literary figure of the day. Some of the most successful of these, remarkable for their delicacy, were produced by Stras at his Paris workshops.

The vogue for wearing bow brooches mimicked current fashions for women, in which dresses were generally covered with large silk bows. Bows were an extraordinarily popular motif, combined with drops in earrings, with miniatures in lockets, or worn around the neck to draw attention to the bosom. Double bows were combined with trembling feathers and flowers in spectacular hair ornaments, while smaller ones were made up into matched sets of pendants and earrings. Today, bows that appear for sale fetch high prices, as the motif remains a popular design, and such pieces, no matter how early, are still bought to be worn. Generally, a bow ornament will sell for

FROM NATURE TO ARTIFICE

■ Brooches which imitated subjects from nature such as this butterfly were always popular, and still command higher prices than less highly sought shapes and motifs. Much of the jewelry from this period was made of white pastes; as a result those pieces which have colored pastes tend to be rarer, and, understandably, more expensive. Butterflies, such as this 18th-century example (*above*, Trevor Allen, London) were firm favorites.

considerably more than a less favored shape of a similar date, as will another enduring favorite, the butterfly. Other shapes taken from nature, such as flowers and insects are also very popular.

The Center of Fashion

Fashions in clothes and jewelry were remarkably similar in both France and England, although France was widely regarded as the leading center for jewelry design and had provided a number of first-class itinerant jewelers who were employed at European courts both north and south. Daytime jewels were generally more restrained than those worn at night, with delicate clusters of paste and gems in subtle colors to match more informal day dresses, or trimmings fashioned into the bows and ribbonwork that were in tune with the rococo style of the time.

Pieces made in France were often more elaborate than their English equivalents, even if they employed the same motifs. Although English pieces could be smaller and simpler, they were just as effective, because of the excellent quality of stones. The *riviére*, a 'river' of stones of the same size or gradually increasing and then decreasing in size to make a perfectly graded necklace, was considered quintessentially English, and was often among the most prestigious jewels that a woman possessed. Riviéres were made in precious stones as well as paste, each stone set in its own tightly fitting mount. Some were sold as a set of separate stones that could be strung on to a ribbon to make a necklace, threaded onto a buckle or used as a set of buttons.

Ornamental buttons were used by both men and women to draw attention to their fashionable attire and became increasingly large toward the end of the 18th century. Many were later converted into cluster brooches, such as this example, *c.* 1800. Harvey & Gore, London.

WAR AND STYLE

The upheaval of war and revolution which haunted much of Europe in the latter part of the 18th century caused a change in jewelry fashions. The emergence of a mass culture helped to supplant precious jewels with sentimental, inexpensive pieces.

Paste was popular with the rich aristocracy not simply because of its high-quality designs and workmanship. Highway robbery was increasingly commonplace during the 18th century; many people therefore had paste copies made of their most valuable jewels, and took these with them when they traveled both at home and abroad. The second half of the century was the time of the Grand Tour, when wealthy, educated English men and women habitually toured the cultural centers of Europe, particularly Germany, France, and Italy, often studying abroad for several years at a time. This penchant for foreign travel was encouraged by the extraordinary discoveries at Herculaneum and Pompeii in 1748 and 1750, when major excavations uncovered Roman ruins; in the case of Pompeii, virtually a whole town. A fervor for classicism swept Europe, bringing with it a movement toward classically inspired lines in architecture, interior decoration, and eventually in jewelry, something of a relief after the fussiness and frivolity of rococo design. In Britain between 1760 and 1785, the distinctive neoclassical Adam style, named after the Scottish-born architect and designer Robert Adam (1728–92), permeated silverware and jewelry alike.

The discoveries in Italy coincided with the first rumblings of discontent at the artifice and frivolity that had so dominated the courts of Europe. These became more clearly heard from the mid-century on, expressed in dissident literature such as the writings of Jean-Jacques Rousseau. His *La Nouvelle Héloïse*, published in 1761, expressed an increasingly widespread feeling that

The classical revival inspired by the discovery of ancient ruins had an effect on all artistic endeavor.

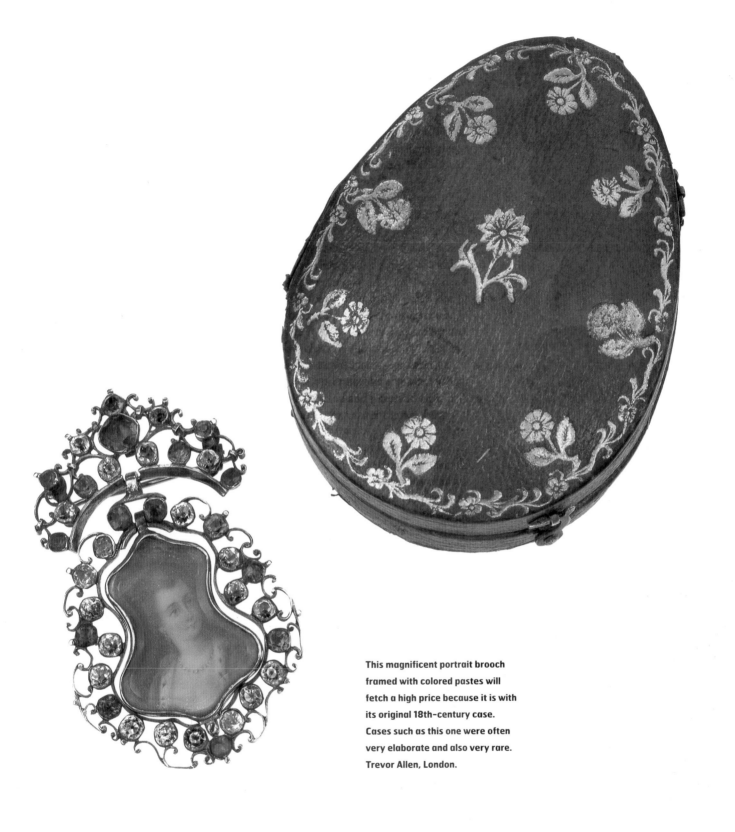

This magnificent portrait brooch
framed with colored pastes will
fetch a high price because it is with
its original 18th-century case.
Cases such as this one were often
very elaborate and also very rare.
Trevor Allen, London.

sentimental values and virtues should be encouraged as an antidote to the artificiality and excess of fashionable life.

Such works encouraged the wearing of sentimental jewelry, especially during the daytime, and before long brooches, rings, bracelets, clasps, and pendants containing locks of hair, or inscribed with loving messages, were worn everywhere. A popular device was to spell out the name of a loved one by the names of the stones, or imitation stones, used in the setting; other pieces were framed with pearls or decorated with enamel. From the mid-17th century, wearing a *memento mori*, a "reminder of death," had been commonplace. Many were made out of gold and enamel and inscribed with mottos such as "in God we trust." These pieces, sometimes referred to as "death jewelry," soon developed into the earliest forms of mourning jewelry, engraved from the middle of the 18th century on with symbols of death such as a skull and crossbones. Memento mori pieces are a good collecting field for those with a strong stomach, as their morbid fascination deters a lot of collectors and pieces can sell for reasonable prices. Most 18th-century pieces, on the other hand, tend to go for sizable sums, their age making them desirable regardless of subject matter. Mourning jewels which refer to specific, well-known personalities also sell well.

As the century progressed, such pieces would often include a lock of hair kept in a case or locket, the compartment inscribed around the outside with an epitaph or the deceased's dates. Lozenge-shaped rings, pendants, and brooches surrounding a sepia miniature were common, as were depictions of mourning muses, or doves representing the Holy Spirit.

A Time of Change

These trinkets were worn alongside grander paste jewels, not in place of them, and the paste trade became increasingly lucrative, with glassmakers jealously defending their sections of the market. Venice cornered the trade in lustrous turquoise pastes, while England continued to supply the most fashionable jewelers such as Stras with the fine lead glass that was so successfully transformed into imitation diamonds. It was not long, however, before the French, prompted by the Académie Royale des Sciences in Paris, began to look for a homemade glass of a similar quality. In 1782, an inquiry into why English-made glass trinkets sold so well in comparison with French ones inspired the French chemist and jeweler Douhault-Wieland to find a

Pinchbeck:
A Substitute for Gold

■ Around 1720, Christopher Pinchbeck (1671–1732), a Fleet Street watch and clock maker, invented a substitute for gold that was remarkably convincing and wore even better than the precious metal itself. With imitation jewelry in mind, Pinchbeck experimented by combining zinc and copper, eventually creating a metal alloy with similar properties to gold and a warm, burnished appearance. Like gold, it was easily worked and could be colored by adding different alloys to the basic recipe. It also combined particularly well with paste, and, given the 18th-century penchant for glitter, before long pinchbeck was widely used and even fashionable. Throughout the late 18th and early 19th centuries until the 1830s, true "pinchbeck," made only by Christopher Pinchbeck and his son, was fashioned into considerable numbers of watches, chatelaines, and tiaras. Some were engraved, others set with paste, but all were distinguished by the highest levels of craftsmanship, even though they were relatively downmarket ornaments in their day.

By 1733 Pinchbeck's invention was already being imitated, both in Britain and in France, and after the mid-19th century the term came to be widely but incorrectly used for any type of gilt metal. It is unusual to come across original pinchbeck" pieces nowadays, but collectors should beware, as unscrupulous or ill-informed dealers still use the term for mid-priced metal alloys, either out of ignorance or in order to raise the price of gilt pieces.

successful glass recipe of his own. By the turn of the 19th century, he was manufacturing paste of such quality that he was exporting stones to Portugal, Spain, Germany, Poland, and Russia.

The success of the paste trade was in a way prophetic, and certainly marked a singular change in social convention. Until paste jewels became so acceptable and successful, there had been a wide gap between the jewels worn by the most wealthy and the trinkets, or poor-quality imitations, worn by those with less money. Jewelry had been a clear indicator of social standing, but suddenly, marquises and middle-class matrons were wearing remarkably similar jewels. Before the end of the 1780s, these hints of social equality were to take a grim turn in France, with the onset of the Revolution (a factor in which was the revival of interest in the democratic principles of the Greeks and Romans, as the struggling working classes grew impatient with their extravagant monarchy.) Even in England, the success of paste on both sides of the class divide suggested a shift in the social structure that was to increase as the century progressed.

With the outbreak of the Revolution in 1789, France's jewelers found themselves out of work. The liberated citizens of the Republic were encouraged to give up their jewels in support of the movement rather than buy new ones, whatever their views in private. Highly decorative jewels were considered suspect, the wearer a threat to the newly established egalitarian regime, and precious gems and pastes were kept firmly out of the public eye. They were replaced in public with gruesome mementoes of the bloodiest decade Europe could remember, such as slivers of blood-red ribbon or a line of small garnets worn like a choker around the neck.

Oval cluster rings such as this 1790s example, set with white paste, were often given as gifts. The underside of this sentimental jewel is inscribed with the word *Amitié*, meaning friendship. Harvey & Gore, London.

Napoleon and Nelson

Once the Revolution was over, ostentation was back, expressed this time in the neoclassical fervor of Napoleon Bonaparte's Directoire and Empire styles. Through the 1790s, fashionable women wore their hair short, in the "Grecian" style. As often as not, the hair was curled and cut around the face, like that of a

This luxurious chatelaine from around 1785 is made of gilt metal, which is often as finely worked as gold. Its small accessories are lined with purple velvet and contain a miniature glass perfume bottle and a thimble. Harvey & Gore, London.

Roman emperor, or alternatively piled high into a classical chignon, with wispy curls on each side of the face. With the arrival of new fabrics from the Far East, including fine gauze, dress styles changed radically. Queen Marie-Antoinette had earlier scandalized French court society by dressing in a simple gauze chemise, then only ever worn as an undergarment. But by the 1790s, such dresses were commonplace among the fashion-conscious, with simple, fluid lines and a high waist just under the armpits.

The most exhibitionist followers of fashion among French women, known ironically as the *merveilleuses* (marvels), wore thin, diaphanous gowns cut exceedingly low at the bust and slit high at the sides. Jewels could be seen around the calves, feet, and thighs, drawing attention to legs covered in flesh-colored tights. The idea of dampening these skimpy dresses to make them cling to the figure became so much the vogue that Parisian doctors issued public warnings to the effect that the practice was life-threatening.

Egyptian Revival

Such costumes were accompanied by paste jewels on aigrettes, this time decorating exotic, North African inspired headdresses, and swathes of gold jewelry, combined with precious and nonprecious stones and other materials. Following the victory of Admiral Horatio Nelson and the British fleet over Napoleon's ships at the 1798 Battle of the Nile, a craze for Egypt swept England, and a frenzy of hero worship for the one-armed, one-eyed naval leader expressed itself in a range of souvenir jewelry, from brooches and medallions to mourning rings on Nelson's death in 1805. Such celebrity worship was on the increase throughout Europe at the end of the 18th century, thanks mainly to improved roads and communications and an increasingly active press. Mass culture was emerging for the first time, as the populations of Europe enjoyed following the exploits of politicians both famous and infamous, war heroes, criminals, artists, writers, and thinkers. Commemorative jewelry was often produced to mark such events.

Gold and Other Metals

Despite the 18th-century passion for diamonds and their imitations, and the consequent rise in popularity of silver as a setting for them, gold remained, as it had always been, a valued precious metal, sought both for its beauty and for its inherent value. Gold chains were worn by both sexes, and women, like men, often wore watches, some of which were much larger than today's equivalents. Watches were an essential accessory for men, especially during the 1770s and 1780s, when they were often worn in pairs; only one would work, while the other, a mock watch, was worn purely as decoration. They were attached to long and often ostentatious gold watch chains, tucked into low coat pockets, and were often decorated with wrought gold seals. Gold rings, too, often doubled as seals.

Women generally hung their engraved, enameled, or bejeweled watches from the waist in a fashion that harked back to the Middle Ages, when aristocratic ladies hung their heavy keys from their belts. Chatelaines, an arrangement of clasps and chains to which various useful household items were attached by a clip, were worn around the waist from the 17th century on. Chatelaines became increasingly decorative during the 18th century, when they were considered an essential part of women's dress. Often beautifully finished, they were strung with a selection of "toys," small, delicately worked tools and knick-knacks such as scissors, thimbles, revolving pencils, or snuff boxes. In many ways, chatelaines served the same purpose as the 20th-century handbag, and remained fashionable until the flimsy, high-waisted dress designs of the late century offered no place to hang them.

Some of the finest chatelaines were made in gold, finished with enameling or set with gems. But cheaper examples were also made, some in the first truly successful imitation of gold, pinchbeck, and others in gilt metal, the

COMMEMORATIVE JEWELRY

■ The advent of wars and revolutions throughout much of late 18th-century Europe, and the ensuing loss of life, provoked a fashion for *memento mori*, or reminders of death. Particularly popular were pendants into which locks of a loved one's hair could be placed. Brooches, rings (*above*, Christie's), bracelets, and clasps were also worn, some inscribed with loving messages, or with the name of the deceased. Religious images and mottos were also commonly used to decorate or inscribe these souvenirs.

techniques of which were first explored from the 18th century on. As chatelaines were such functional objects, they were made in great numbers, especially the more downmarket ones. The finest are expensive to collect today, but gilt metal or silver housekeeping chatelaines from the late 18th and early 19th centuries come up for sale regularly, and are reasonably priced.

Cut Steel

Steel also provided inspiration for jewelers. Steelworking had been a recognized trade since the 16th century, but in the first years of the 18th century, a Mr. Metcalfe organized the cottage-industry producers of steelwork at Woodstock, near Oxford, England, into an efficient business. Within 30 years the Woodstock workers were producing delicate, well-finished accessories for the nobility, such as scissors, watch chains, and

Matthew Boulton, Artist and Industrialist

■ The Birmingham mass-production trade in cut steel jewelry and trinkets, or "toys," gave rise to one of the century's greatest British industrialists, Matthew Boulton (1728–1809). Boulton inherited his father's toymaking business in 1759 and set about improving declining standards. By 1770, he had turned the business round, employing up to 800 people to make high-class cut steel toys at his new factory at Soho, Birmingham, which he ran with John Fothergill.

From the 1760s on, cut steel was combined to great effect with another diamond substitute, marcasite, a naturally shiny metallic substance of a gunmetal gray cut from the mineral iron pyrites. When faceted, polished, and set, marcasite glitters like diamonds. Its popularity started in the 1770s and 80s, especially in Switzerland, where the wearing of diamonds was forbidden by sumptuary laws (laws governing the lavishness of dress according to rank). Marcasite was usually set in silver or pewter and was often combined with enamel into beautifully crafted, expensive ornaments that were worn by all levels of society. Boulton used marcasite with cut steel on a range of belts, buttons, earrings, bracelets, pendants, and chatelaines.

These glittering luxuries were so fine that by the 1780s cut steel had become extremely fashionable, and was correspondingly expensive to buy. In 1767, the English Queen Charlotte, wife of George III, yielded to the vogue for elegant steel jewelry, and

Matthew Boulton was charged to make her two cut steel chains, each of which would have taken months to complete. Fashionable women and courtiers followed her example, donning bracelets, mesh chains, necklaces, and chatelaines. Many of these were produced at Boulton's factory and were exported throughout Europe, along with the steel buttons for which he was particularly renowned, and that were essential wear for the well-dressed 18th-century gentleman.

Boulton was not known for his cut steel alone, however. The first copper pennies ever struck in Britain, in 1797, came from his factory, and he was also the country's leading producer of Sheffield plate. In the early 19th century, Boulton went on to combine his remarkable talents with another innovative English producer, the renowned potter Josiah Wedgwood combining cut steel with cameos on jewelry, toys, and other pieces.

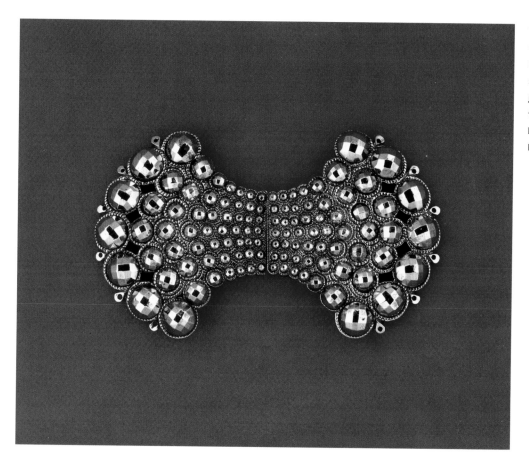

medals. There was also a thriving trade in shoe buckles, and when these went out of style in the late 18th century, the steelworkers turned their attention to cut steel, cutting the soft bluish metal into faceted, blue-gray "stones" or studs that were found to glint and sparkle when lit, in the fashion so beloved of the time. Before long, these steel studs were being turned into gleaming bracelets and necklaces, riveted onto a shaped back plate cut from a sheet of brass or low-grade silver. Steel sequins and steel embroidery were popular, too, sewn onto dresses and capes.

Imitators of the Oxfordshire enterprise sprang up all over England, and one of their most successful rivals was the firm run by Matthew Boulton, which he inherited from his father in the mid-century. Boulton was so successful at raising standards that it is hard to distinguish the mass-produced cut steel trinkets made by his company from the home-crafted pieces that emerged from the Woodstock cottage industry. Cut steel was combined with other materials, too, from Staffordshire enamels to the ceramic plaques made by Wedgwood. Many such pieces encased cameo-like portraits of characters and events from history, especially the antiquities that were so fashionable at the time, and reflected the literary concerns of the day.

Supporting the War Effort

In part, the popularity of jewels made from nonprecious materials was due to a need to contribute to national campaigns and wars. More expensive pieces of jewelry were either broken down and reworked, or melted down for the value of their gold. Jewels made from steel and crystal, on the other hand, had little intrinsic worth, but they were valued as objects that were attractive in design rather than the materials they were made from. This was indicative of things to come, as the movement toward mass production continued and the rigid social structures that had been in place in Europe for hundreds of years began to crumble. Jewelry, as with other areas of the arts, reflected these changes, as the qualities inherent in cheaper materials were recognized for the first time.

CHAPTER TWO

The Age of Sentiment

Stylish jewels became affordable for all classes of society as advances in industry led to mass production and cheaper goods. New types of stone were discovered and quickly copied into paste, particularly into the sentimental jewelry that a new spirit of romanticism inspired. Cut steel and jet became popular and there was a revival in cameos, inspired by interest in classical art. But industrialization brought about the most significant changes in costume jewelry.

FRENCH JEWELRY REVIVED

After the austerity imposed by the Revolution, French jewelers welcomed the influence of Napoleon's empress, Joséphine, who loved fine clothes and jewelry. Paste, cameos, and cut steel all enjoyed favor as jewelers set about to revive forgotten skills.

The move toward classicism that had begun in the 1750s gathered momentum in the first years of the 19th century. What had begun as an intellectual movement 50 years earlier transformed itself into popular culture, spurred on by the fascination, if not approval, that all Europe felt for Napoleon Bonaparte and his exploits. Following Napoleon's coronation as Emperor of France in 1804, the newly restored French aristocracy once again began to flaunt its wealth, and the market for jewelry revived.

The flimsy Directoire gowns of the 1790s remained fashionable; gold bangles were worn on bare arms, one high up, one at the elbow, and another at the wrist, often decorated with typically neoclassical motifs such as laurel wreaths, doves, or Greek key patterns. Rings were worn on every finger, including the thumb. Although hairstyles were no longer eccentrically enormous as in the 18th century, they were still lavishly decorated with combs and tiaras fashioned out of precious metals and set with stones. But above all, the society woman in the period of Napoleon's Empire bedecked herself in chains, slung across the body or around the neck. One fashion, a series of short gold neck-chains, was called *en esclavage* (in slavery) while others made a feature of gold mesh rather than simple gold links.

The decadence of France's Napoleonic era was aped, rather than spurned, by the Bourbon kings once they were returned to power in 1815, although the severity of Empire design was abandoned in favor of the grandiose Restoration style that looked back to the rococo curves of the

The necklace with oval pink pastes mounted on pinchbeck (*top left*) dates from 1820. Religious fervor in Europe during the early 18th century resulted in jewels of a religious nature such as this decorative paste pendant cross (*top right*) c. 1820. The paste brooch (*bottom left*) c. 1875, in the shape of a crescent, uses one of the oldest motifs in jewelry design. Harvey & Gore, London. The delicate *verre églomisé* bracelet (*bottom right*) set in gilt metal dates from c. 1830. Beauty & the Beasts, London.

18th century. These trends were copied in England, where the 18th-century tradition of displaying wealth through large, ostentatious gemstones was still firmly in place. The Prince Regent, later to become George IV, spent more on jewels than any English monarch since Henry VIII. Consequently, diamonds and other precious stones were still greatly sought, and the larger the better.

Although the wars with Napoleonic France, fought on and off between 1792 and 1815, kept the English at home, the booming wartime economy led to an ever-wealthier middle class, obsessed with keeping abreast of the latest court fashions. As in France, light, short-sleeved gauze dresses with low necklines and high waists were accompanied by hair dressed in Grecian topknots, while English men followed the lead of Beau Brummell, friend of the Prince Regent and arbiter of taste, in wearing clean-cut coats and trousers and exaggerated cravats. During the brief spells of peace, rich

Cameo Fervor

■ Although the catalyst for the popularity of cameos was the taste for the neoclassical in the early 19th century, the fascination with antique Greek and Roman cameos of shell or stone started with the discoveries of Roman ruins 50 or so years before. Most of them were single-color examples carved out of hardstone, ivory, or coral, or two-color shell cameos, with the relief carving in a different color from the background. More unusual pieces had three or four layers of varying colors.

As truly antique examples were rare and expensive, it was not long before contemporary imitations were being made, some as fakes, most as straightforward reproductions, such as the Italian 19th-century cameo (*above*, Christie's). The unglazed jasperware cameos made from 1775 on in Britain by the Staffordshire potter Josiah Wedgwood (1730–95) came into this category, as did the skillful glass cameos of the Scotsman James Tassie

(1735–99). Wedgwood carved the easily tinted white stoneware against a variety of colored backgrounds. Tassie successfully marketed great numbers of his glass cameos, which were soon widely copied. Although original Tassies are rarely for sale today, collections of Tassie-style glass cameos are available from time to time, usually sold as a group.

Cameos carved in workshops around Rome and Naples were more downmarket, designed as souvenir jewelry and sold in quantity to tourists and travelers on the Grand Tour during the 18th and 19th centuries. Many such cameos were crudely carved and bought unmounted, to be set with varying degrees of skill once the tourists returned home. As the 19th century progressed, cameos were increasingly mass-produced by stencil carving, resulting in stiff, angular reliefs that are easy to tell from earlier, better-made examples.

Among the most collectible of these Grand Tour cameos were those produced in the workshops of the Saulini family in Rome. Many of their cameos were signed, and these are now the most highly sought of this date, fetching high prices when they come up for sale. Any signature adds value to a cameo, and is usually found on the truncation (below the head and shoulders) at the front or scratched into the back.

It is worth keeping an eye open for fakes, as some are very skillfully produced and hard to spot. A common ploy was to carve the cameo layers from separate pieces of stone and join them together. To check for this, look along the sides of the cameo for any seams. Another tip is to check that the mount and the cameo are of similar quality. If a good carving is set in a cheap metal mount, be suspicious.

English families would visit the continent; otherwise, they would amuse themselves with a social whirl of visits to spa towns, country houses, and seaside resorts. With them would travel a generous selection of both precious and costume jewels, usually set in the classical style. These jewels combined colored stones as varied as topaz, aquamarine, amethyst, peridot, turquoise, and chrysoprase, or their paste equivalents, with gold mounts that looked deceptively substantial. In fact, as gold was rare and expensive, most mounts were made from sheets of gold hammered very thin and shaped into hollow-backed settings. Being more fragile than they seemed, they were easily damaged.

Joséphine and the Jewelers

In France, extravagance was an understandable reaction against the restrictions of the Revolutionary years. One of those who had chafed under the need for restraint in the previous decade was Joséphine de Beauharnais, a beautiful and charming Creole woman who had spent a considerable number of years in prison during the Revolution, but who had survived against all odds (her first husband was guillotined in July 1794). Joséphine's name was linked with a number of important Revolutionary figures before she finally married Napoleon Bonaparte in 1796, on the advice, it is said, of her lover, Paul Barras, and threw herself into public life. Hailed as "Our Lady of Victories," she indulged her passion for clothes and jewels, and was a godsend to the ailing French jewelry trade. Joséphine was as well-known and influential in her day as the actress Sarah Bernhardt was to become at the start of the 20th century, and through her the wearing of jewelry became once again the height of fashion.

During the dark years of terror, apprenticeships in goldsmithing had been abolished, because it was a trade that had so blatantly catered for the ruling classes. There was little work for goldsmiths other than melting down jewels from a more extravagant era in order to fill the coffers of the new Revolutionary councils. The consequent lack of training inevitably led to lower standards of workmanship, but also opened up the possibilities for invention, freeing new jewelers from earlier methods of working. The range of jewels produced widened to include more purely whimsical pieces, purposely designed to accompany a particular fashion.

Paste Rivals Diamonds

As in the previous century, a passion for gemstones gave a tremendous boost to the trade in paste jewelry. Harlequin paste, which combined many different colored glass stones in a single piece, emerged in the first years of the 19th century, its characteristically soft colors created with different foils. Paste of this date was still set in closed mounts, backed with thin cups of silver or gold. At the same time, however, as early as 1800, it was discovered that open settings allowed more light to shine through the stones and improved their sparkle. This method of setting was eventually adopted for most stones, whether precious or paste, although it is unusual to find paste pieces in open settings made before 1830–40. Such a time lag between advances in precious stone setting and paste is fairly normal, and can give a clue to the date of a piece. Tiaras, earrings, necklaces, bracelets, brooches, single or in parures, in fashionable shapes, colors, and materials, were avidly sought at smart Parisian jewelers' stores. One store, Au Petit Dunkerque, owned by M. Granchez and fashionably situated on the Quai de Conti, became the place to be seen for the most influential leaders of fashion and style. Queen Marie Antoinette had been a customer at M. Granchez's establishment, and others had flourished in the 18th century, but they had faded during the Revolution. Now, the renewed interest in jewels and trinkets of all types, bought for novelty value or as gifts, brought the trade back to life, the best of the paste commanding a price to rival that of diamonds.

Joséphine Bonaparte's extravagant passion for jewels led to the revival of the ailing French jewelry trade after she married France's hero Napoleon Bonaparte.
Corbis-Bettmann, London.

OPALINE GLASS JEWELRY

■ Early in the century, opaline glass jewelry, which was produced primarily at Uttoxeter in Staffordshire, England, became extremely fashionable for daytime wear, being quieter and less flamboyant than evening jewels. The soft tints of opal were imitated by backing the semi-opaque glass with a pink foil, and the resulting pastes were worked into jewels of all sorts, decorated with bows, butterflies, chandelier shapes, and flowers. Opaline glass jewelry is not common today, and a well-made pair of earrings or a necklace can fetch a high price. It is worth buying, as it is a collecting area which has been largely ignored in the past. But beware: original opaline glass is very similar in color to a less attractive glass produced in the early 1900s.

VAUXHALL GLASS

■ Vauxhall glass was a novelty of the early part of the 18th century in Britain. Its name came from the early mirror glass made at a glassworks owned by the Duke of Buckingham in Vauxhall, London, from the late 17th century on. Its hard, shiny quality made Vauxhall glass easy to cut, foil, and set, like other glass paste. Up to the 1830s, Vauxhall glass trinkets were exceedingly popular, often made of a deep Burgundy-red glass that was shaped into flower necklaces, insect brooches, earrings, and hair ornaments. The black glass insect brooch (*above*, Beauty & the Beasts, London) dates from the late 19th century and reflects the fascination for anything gruesome, macabre, or just plain creepy that prevailed at the time. Some pieces were made entirely of glass, others were combined with gilt metal. Early pieces of Vauxhall glass are rare and valuable, as little of it has survived unscathed.

Although the cut steel trade started in England, it flourished in France in the early 19th century. Good pieces such as this parure (*right*) are very valuable today. The stunning pinchbeck and gilt metal parure (*opposite page*) was probably made in England, *c.* 1825. Large buckles were newly fashionable, drawing attention to a narrow waistline, and several bracelets would have been worn at one time. Madeleine Popper, London.

The taste for all things neoclassical was reflected in another jewelry craze that seized the imagination in both France and Britain, and was to last for 80 years or more. Antique cameos were first studied as an intellectual pursuit, but by the turn of the century this interest had filtered through to the jewelry trade. By 1804 or so, Parisian women were wearing cameos in every conceivable setting and combination, singly or grouped together, some matched in pairs of earrings or brooches, others strung together to make cameo necklaces or bracelets. Cameos adorned hair combs, belt buckles, hat jewels, and rings, and the more that could be worn together, the better.

The French Vogue for Cut Steel

Another popular establishment in Paris was Deferney, a firm of costume jewelry makers with a store at 243 Place du Palais Royale, where the cream of French society shopped for ornaments of all kinds. The business dealt above all in cut steel, an English specialty that had been adopted in France during a late 18th-century spasm of Anglomania. It had in fact been established there in the 1780s by an Englishman, Mr. Sykes, when he moved to Paris from Yorkshire.

Cut steel was generally very expensive in comparison to paste. Its sparkle was reminiscent of diamonds, but it was appreciated as a material in its own right. Cut steel studs were often combined with semiprecious stones such as moss agate or cornelian, and set in geometric, neoclassical styles. Deferney was known for its jewels and fancy goods in both cut steel and paste, and was commissioned by Napoleon's second Empress, Marie-Louise, to make a cut steel set of comb, chains, and bracelet. Cut steel's place in the affections of

the French was assured following the 1819 design exhibition held in Paris. Flamboyant cut steel jewelry, much cheaper than before, was presented at the exhibition by a manufacturer named Frichot, who had invented a mechanical device to cut and shape the metal. Before long, his firm was employing almost 2,000 workers to supply the huge demand for his money bags, parures, flower brooches, and decorative buckles worn around the neck or on hats, bags, and purses.

The popularity of cut steel went from strength to strength, with firms such as Henriet and Schey in France, and Boulton in England producing quantities of high-quality brooches, elegant earrings that reflected the light, finely-wrought necklaces, bangles of steel studs and flexible bracelets of fine wire mesh. Cut steel combs and aigrettes, designed to decorate carefully coiffed hair, used a range of charming motifs, many of them hinting at the more romantic mood that was to sweep Europe as the century progressed. Miniature sparkling insects, stars, flowers, butterflies, birds, and plants lit up the dazzling array of cut steel jewels, with the fleur-de-lys a particular favorite in France and the padlock, found mainly on bracelets, in England.

Many wealthy people traveled widely in the 19th century, often taking in recently discovered Roman ruins on their way. *Pietra dura*, or hardstone mosaic jewelry such as this were often among the mementos they took home with them. Trevor Allen, London.

THE NEW WAVE OF ROMANTICISM

A new wave of sentiment and romanticism swept Europe, partly in response to the horrors of revolution and war. But literature, the Far East, and ancient civilizations began to influence jewelry design.

A pinchbeck mounted bracelet, *c.* 1825, has set circular amethysts with pearl set star centers. Harvey & Gore, London.

The close contact between Britain and France was upset by the shocking events of the Revolution, when the rich and aristocratic were terrified that similar changes would sweep the British Isles. The Napoleonic Wars further widened the gulf. Ideas and fashions nevertheless continued to be exchanged between the two countries. Paris was still considered the leader of fashion, and English polite society looked to France for its lead, avidly consuming editions of *Le Cabinet des Modes* with its engraved fashion plates, a journal that had first been published in France in 1785. French dress styles were adopted in Britain, but in more modest versions. Low necklines were draped with cashmere shawls or fichus, while the narrow, high-waisted dresses, in soft fabrics and pale colors, were rarely as transparent, or split so high at the sides, as those worn by the most daring of exhibitionist French ladies. Cottons and other fabrics imported from India and beyond by the East India companies had a considerable influence on English styles, which were often eclectic, combining fringed shawls with turbans.

Many pieces of restrained daytime jewelry began to show traces of a trend toward romanticism and sentiment. Natural shapes such as flowers and plants started to be more realistically designed than before, with more movement in the setting. Colorful brooches and pins fashioned into pansies, birds, butterflies, and insects, among many other forms, began to be produced in great numbers. By the 1820s, informal dress and jewelry styles were moving in a new direction. The romantic ideals which first appeared in the writings of the first quarter of the century, most notably the ballads and poems by the Scottish author Sir Walter Scott (1771–1832), were widely adopted after the 1814 publication of Scott's first historical novel, *Waverley*, and his subsequent works. Before long, fashionable women who were thrilled by the spine-chilling Gothic novels that they read to pass the time of day were wearing tight-waisted dresses with billowing sleeves that harked back to medieval or Renaissance designs, as well as buying any number of small pieces of sentimental jewelry.

Scott was not the only author to inspire the Romantic movement, which quickly spread through all echelons of society. In 1822, the French writer Chateaubriand was amazed to find the Empress Marie-Louise, by then Napoleon's widow, wearing chips of marble set in gold when he visited her in Verona; the marble was said to have been taken from the tomb of Juliet, Shakespeare's tragic young heroine.

By the 1830s, romanticism was in full swing, fueled by patriotism and nostalgia, both prevalent in the literature of the day. Jewelry design, like other areas, drew its influences from countless different sources, including a new fervor for religion that spawned early Gothic designs. The religious revival took hold throughout Europe from early in the century, when, for the first time since the Renaissance, it became commonplace for men and women to wear items of religious jewelry such as crosses and rosaries. Many of these were made in the newly fashionable Berlin ironwork, a material felt to symbolize solid constancy and durability. Miniatures of saints were framed and worn as lockets, and rosary rings became essential wear for the devout.

The Gothic styles popular from the 1820s on were first seen in costume jewelry in the form of large belt buckles, some made of Berlin ironwork, others of cut steel, pinchbeck or numerous alloys or gilt metals. The buckles might sport medieval architectural features such as arches or trefoils, or feature as a centerpiece pilgrims kneeling at a shrine. Their size and design drew attention to a waist that was fashionably small, especially after tight-waisted gowns were reintroduced in the 1830s and 1840s.

The Romantic Style

In the early years of the century, Far Eastern and ancient European civilizations continued to influence makers of both precious and costume jewelry, who were particularly excited by the large hoards of Etruscan jewelry found in tombs on the outskirts of Rome in the 1830s. These soon gave rise to an "archeological style," much of which incorporated the granulation and filigree work typical of Etruscan ornaments, and by the mid-19th century Europe was struck by a craze for Etruscan *bullae* (pendants which hung from a band around the neck), Roman pins and *fibulae* (arm bracelets), amulets, and Greek daggers. Many of these were decorated with shell and glass mosaic inspired by Roman architectural detail, while others incorporated cameos. In the mid-century, Roman coin settings also became fashionable, worn around the neck or in a set with matching earrings, although much of the work was heavy-handed, relying on thick mounts of gold for its effect. Small, enameled paintings of scenes from Pompeii strung together into necklaces or included on headbands were typical of Pompeiian-style jewelry, much of which was bought by travelers in southern Italy. So widely worn was this jewelry, which often mixed Roman, Greek, and

The romantic revival of the mid-18th century prompted an interest in openly religious jewelry such as this gilt pendant cross set with pastes.
Beauty & the Beasts, London.

A micromosaic brooch, *c.* 1860, depicting various birds, would have been a popular memento of a European Grand Tour. These mosaics often used flowers, animals or other motifs from nature as subjects, in imitation of classical mosaics. Beauty & the Beasts.

Colored pastes surround the face on this exquisite buckle clock of about 1820. The movement was made by the well-known clock makers William Ballentine of Cable Street, in the City of London. Harvey & Gore, London.

Etruscan motifs in a single piece, that it was satirized by the British magazine *Punch*. Its June 1859 edition contained a cartoon entitled "A young lady on the High Classical School of Ornament," which poked fun at young English women and their craze for such jewelry. Thanks to its popularity at the time, such pieces are still in circulation today, and can be picked up easily from dealers and auction houses.

Within the elitist circles of the truly rich, hair and neck jewels continued to hold pride of place in a woman's jewel box. Tiaras were topped with plumes of ostrich feathers, held in place by a jeweled comb which matched long earrings. Bouquets of flowers, stalks of wheat, fluttering butterflies, delicate moths were attached to the side of the head, and moved gently with the wearer on trembler springs.

Inspired by the Crusades, a rash of toques and turbans came into fashion, again pinned in place with sparkling brooches of paste, shaped into Islamic crescents or imitation feathers. Hair was generally worn up, with long earrings to balance it, matching a cross or brooch at the center of the low neckline. The chandelier-shaped girandole earrings came back into vogue,

In "regard" rings such as this, the choice of stones would spell out a message. In this ring from 1810, the paste equivalents of rubies, emeralds, garnets, amethysts, rubies again, and diamonds have been used. Harvey & Gore, London.

The American Costume Jewelry Trade

■ Up to the second half of the 19th century, there was little or no tradition of American jewelers working with precious metals or stones. The wealthy of New York and other important cities would travel to Europe to buy their jewels. Diamonds, highly popular in Europe in the 18th and 19th centuries, were exported to the United States for the first time only after 1850 or so. The bulk of the American jewelry trade was faux or imitation jewelry, copies of upscale pieces, and costume jewelry, trinkets, and ornaments were designed to be cheerful and decorative rather than having any artistic or inherent value. Such jewelry was common, and as long as it was cheap enough, sold in considerable quantities; few New World pioneers had large amounts of cash to spare.

Unlike Europe, where jewelry was usually made in small, family-run businesses, most American jewelry was made by large companies such as Tiffany's, which did not really come to prominence until the early 20th century. By the 1850s, it, and others, had established factories in Providence, Rhode Island, with a considerable output. It was very common for the same design to be produced in several different versions: a pure gold piece made for the top end of

the market, a cheaper, rolled-gold plate copy for the middle-income bracket, and, for those with the least to spend, a stamped brass version, which was then electroplated with a miniscule scrap of gold to give it an air of luxury.

Much of the mass-produced American jewelry could be manufactured very cheaply because of the technique of plating, in which a base metal is covered with a small amount of a more precious one. Known as Sheffield plate in England, it was developed by Thomas Bolsover of Sheffield in the 1740s, when he found out how to fuse a thin layer of silver onto a sheet of copper by heating and then rolling them together. In Providence, Rhode Island, this technique, slightly modified, was known as sweat plating. In the early 19th century, the principle was applied to gold: copper sheets and thin copper wire were coated with a small amount of the precious metal to make rolled gold. This inexpensive material was then transformed into countless items of cheap jewelry

American pieces can be hard to spot, although anything stamped "gold filled" (rolled gold) is definitely made in the United States. Makers' marks tended to be of a different type from those of their European counterparts. Most French and English jewelers stamped their work with their initials, while American craftsmen were more likely to use a graphic of some sort, such as an arrow, accompanied by the carat (grade) of the metal.

Sparkling paste tiaras such as this
white paste 1830s example were
regularly worn by wealthy women
and remained fashionable to the
end of the century and beyond.
Harvey & Gore, London .

along with elongated pendants that contained subtle references to events of
the time, such as a naval battle. Women who favored the romantic style of
dressing, at least during the daytime, donned flowing gowns with billowing
sleeves, and hung a brightly colored Geneva watch from the tightly drawn-in
waist. Arms were covered from wrist to elbow with wide gold bracelets,
fastened with the ubiquitous Renaissance motif of a pair of clasping hands, or
sometimes with a clasp that opened to reveal a miniature of a friend or
relative. Large clasps were typical, often set with cut stones and intricately
worked with leaves or scrolls.

Long gold and pinchbeck chains hung round the neck, often hooked in at
the waist, sometimes strung with large crosses, or ending in lorgnettes
(eyeglasses) or vinaigrettes (smelling bottles). Recently, such chains have
been reproduced in large numbers, and collectors need to be wary about
paying high prices. It is hard to spot modern pieces, although the different
methods of casting are the best clue. The wisest course is to buy from auction
houses or dealers that you know and trust. They will be more likely to take
the piece back if it turns out to be a modern reproduction.

This enamel and gilt bracelet made
in Switzerland in the 19th century
reflects the romantic interests of
the day with its tiny pictures of
distant follies and ruins.
Trevor Allen, London.

Large belt buckles such as this
19th-century oval colored paste
buckle (*right*) *c.* 1875, adorned the
cinched waists that became
popular during the period.
Harvey & Gore, London.

The Appeal of Sentiment

Many 19th-century sentimental jewels are particularly charming, decorated with recurrent motifs of more or less universal appeal. A lock of hair, or a portrait of a lover or relative, was incorporated into brooches, lockets, rings, necklaces, and pendants. The snake, often coiled with its tail in its mouth to form a ring or bangle, was understood to signify both wisdom and eternity, and was the most frequently used decorative motif of the time on both men's and women's jewels. Unmistakable tokens of love, from hearts to lock-and-key jewels, were produced in huge quantities, while many jewels set with real or imitation stones contained a hidden message in the choice of stone. Rubies, emeralds, garnets, amethysts, rubies again, and diamonds, or their paste equivalents, would spell out "REGARD," for example, while others might be inscribed with the word *amitié*, friendship, on the back of the setting. In some cases, what appears to be a "regard" ring or jewel does not seem to spell the word correctly. This is because some semiprecious stones were known by different names: garnet was often called "violetta."

THE ERA OF INDUSTRIALIZATION

True industrialization, improved production techniques, and great social change, meant that the demand for costume jewelry soared. But mass production led to a backlash in jewelry design, resulting in a revival of interest in "art" jewels.

By the time Queen Victoria ascended the British throne in 1837, fashions in jewelry were changing with dizzying speed. Women of the period decked themselves in clanking, amusing jewels and trinkets to accompany colorful, romantic styles of dress for daytime wear. Fashions were so fleeting that there was just time for a maid to acquire a cheap imitation of her mistress's jewels before they went out of favor. This confusion and profusion of styles became the hallmark of Victorian design.

Such an eclectic approach to fashion and style was encouraged by significant advances in industrialization, both inside and outside the jewelry trade. As the century progressed, jewelers saw their business change drastically as machines began to take the place of skilled craftsmen. Although the rich continued to buy handcrafted pieces of great value, either precious or paste, industrialization brought in its wake a greatly enriched general population, keen to spend their wealth on mass-produced objects. The ancient arts of casting metals and stamping designs out of thin metallic sheets were everyday methods of making jewelry at the start of the century. But before long they were outmoded, abandoned in favor of the far quicker, and therefore more economical production techniques made possible with machines driven by gas and steam. These new methods of manufacturing led to vastly increased competition. For the first time, independent designers who were not themselves goldsmiths became involved in the production of jewels, headhunted by rival firms of costume jewelers anxious to maintain their grip on the growing market with a stream of original and fashionable designs.

The effect of mass production showed itself most clearly on earrings. The flowing hairstyles of the 1840s and 50s meant that earrings fell out of favor for 20 years or so, and few were made. When in the 1860s a return to wearing the hair up created a fresh demand, the market was swamped with vast quantities of pendant earrings in innumerable designs. Many were the result of designers investigating the possibilities of Machine Age tools, playing with

Queen Victoria (*above*) reigned over the British Empire for much of the 19th century and had a tremendous impact on jewelry fashion. The wearing of mourning jewelry, jet in particular, was given a boost by her adherence to the conventions of the day.

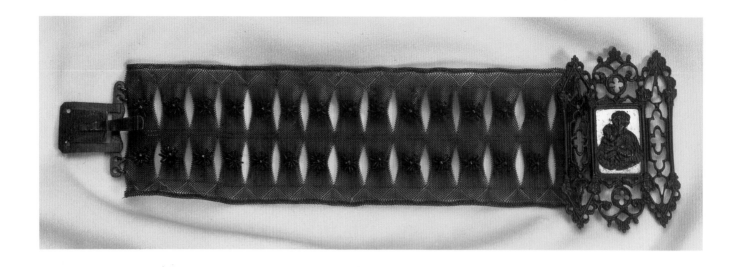

National Pride in Berlin Ironwork

■ Late in the 18th century, there was a drop in demand for the cast-iron products that the iron industry of Prussia (now northeastern Germany) had long exported all over Europe. The skilled and experienced armorers and ironfounders for which the industry was famous were no longer required, and were facing unemployment. Two of them, Friedrich Anton Freiherr and Friedrich Wilhelm von Reden from Gleiwitz, Silesia, determined not to see their livelihood slip away, experimented with the consistency of the molten iron to see if it could be used to cast more delicate wares. Once they had developed a thinner liquid, they combined forces with a British engineer by the name of Wilkinson. In the mid-1790s, the three set up the Gleiwitz Foundry, which by 1798 was making cast-iron cameos and medals, among other pieces. It was not long before their wares were highly sought, especially once they exhibited at the Royal Academy of Arts and Mechanical Sciences in Berlin in 1804. The following year, the factory made more than 6,500 cameos. The skilled Prussian ironworkers turned their hand to other pieces as well; the mesh on the 1820s bracelet (*above*, Madeleine Popper, London) is testament to their craftsmanship.

Inevitably, its success was soon copied. The small decorative wares, especially jewelry, made by the Royal Berlin Foundry became the most desirable, and the foundry gave its name to the style. The austere blackness of cast-iron jewelry was ideally suited to mourning wear, and following the death of

Queen Luisa of Prussia in 1810, small iron crosses were frequently worn as a mark of respect.

The trade received an enormous boost around 1813, when funds were raised to pay for the wars against Napoleon and the French, and wealthy Prussians were asked to turn in their gold jewelry for the sake of the nation. In return, they were given a piece of iron jewelry, often a cross, that was inscribed and dated, sometimes commemorating a particular battle.

Although a minor decorative iron industry did become established in France after Napoleon invaded Prussia in 1807, most Berlin ironwork continued to be made in and around the Prussian capital until the mid-century. Many jewels were fashioned out of panels of slender cast iron linked together into bracelets, necklaces, and crosses, often with the most delicate of fretwork. Others incorporated distinctive black and white cameos. Much of the ironwork was eclectic in its subject matter, combining elements of neoclassical design with Gothic arches or tracery and more romantic themes; the most upscale of the pieces were finished with gold.

Pieces are most valuable today if they are signed by the best-known makers, including Siméon Pierre Deveranne (1789–1859), a French-born goldsmith whose Berlin foundry exhibited all over Europe and exported copious quantities of romantic cameo pieces with historical and literary themes to England; Johann Conrad Philipp Geiss (1772–1846), whose work was renowned for its open lacework decoration; and Karl Friedrich Schinkel (1781–1841), who specialized from the 1830s in Gothic-influenced wrought-iron jewels. Other makers to look out for include August Ferdinand Lehmann, Hossauer, and Edward Schott of Ilsenburg. The most collectible Berlin ironwork pieces are sets with their original cases, since they are less likely to have rusted over the years.

light and shape rather than depending on the quality of materials for their effect. Buying earrings of this date can be costly. Pairs are relatively rare, as people tend to lose a single earring, and they are normally bought to be worn rather than displayed. Dating earrings from this time can be hard; many of the designs were remarkably advanced in style and could have been made some 50 years later. Good examples can change hands for very high prices.

Well-established centers of costume jewelry, such as Pforzheim in Germany, Birmingham in England, Gablonz in Bohemia, and later, Providence, Rhode Island, were ideally placed to make the most of these new mechanical production techniques. They flooded the market with reproductions of the upscale jewels that were still being turned out by goldsmiths and gemcutters in Europe and farther afield.

The Purist Backlash

Before long, however, purist craftsmen in both the United States and in Europe were objecting to the poor workmanship inevitably found in cheap, mass-produced jewels. In Europe, a backlash against this cheap jewelry caused a renewed interest in "peasant" jewelry, held to be more honest and solid than the products of the Industrial Revolution. This rejection of industrial progress found its voice in the English artist and designer William Morris (1834–96) and his associates, who argued that mass-produced goods had neither soul nor artistic merit, and impoverished the lives of those who lived among them. In sympathy, many educated women stopped wearing jewelry, or abandoned "industrial" jewels for the more expensive "art" jewels of Italian makers such as Fortunato Pio Castellani (1794–1865), who established the influential Greek and Etruscan styles. Those who could not afford Castellani's pieces did not need to wait long until cheaper imitations appeared on the market.

Art jewels were not the only form of upscale jewel on sale. Diamonds had never gone out of style for the rich and famous, nor had paste, especially among the aristocracies of Europe. The French jeweler Olivier Massin (born 1829, retired 1892) came up with a way of creating a realistically quivering flower by threading its "stem," made of a series of tubes, onto a length of steel spring. The effect was so successful that it was soon used in all sorts of large jewels, from hair ornaments to corsage pieces, in precious as well as paste jewelry. From the 1860s on, all manner of natural forms were produced *en tremblant* (trembling), winged insects such as flies, butterflies, and dragonflies, and the large, grotesque beetle brooches that were especially popular in France.

Unwittingly, the 19th-century explorers who set out in search of new lands had a profound effect on jewelry design. Many insect brooches were made with newly discovered gemstones. These included the green demantoid

The Roman art jeweler Fortunato Pio Castellani (1794–1865) often made art pieces from nonprecious metals, such as this gilt metal brooch, but his ideas were widely copied. Beauty & the Beasts, London.

Hair ornaments were often made *en tremblant*, created in such a way that their wings or bodies moved with the wearer. Beauty & the Beasts, London.

This mourning jewel contains carefully preserved locks of hair from the person the brooch remembers. The dates of the person on the back indicate that it was made in 1853. Beauty & the Beasts, London.

garnets that were first discovered in Siberia in the 1860s which went on to become very fashionable later in the century. These stones had a remarkable depth to them, with the fire of a diamond and an even brighter green than the peridot. Sometimes the color was so strong that they were used in place of emeralds. Golden-brown crocidolite, or tiger's eye, was found in southwestern Africa, black opals were unearthed on Lightning Ridge, Queensland, Australia, and sapphires were found in Kashmir, where they were used by the local population as gun flints. Rubies were exhaustively mined in Burma, while fresh supplies of gold were struck in California, Australia, and South Africa. Before long, paste copies of all the new gems were readily available to costume jewelers.

The Commercialization of Grief

Queen Victoria's accession to the throne of Great Britain at the tender age of 18 was considered as romantic as any of the novels that she read in her youth, and when she married Prince Albert of Saxe-Coburg in 1840, it was as if a fairy tale had come true. She was a woman of her time, sticking rigidly to etiquette and always following mourning rituals, which became increasingly elaborate as the century progressed. It was no surprise that when Prince Albert died of typhoid in 1861, the whole country was drawn into the queen's personal tragedy as she embraced her grief wholeheartedly. A thriving trade

Bog oak, dug out of Irish marshland, was also used for mourning jewels. This brooch from 1860 depicts a castle. Beauty & the Beasts, London.

The Passion for Jet

■ Jet ornaments from ancient civilizations, some dating back to the Bronze Age and before, can only be admired in museums, but 19th-century jet, produced in large quantities as mourning jewelry, is still widely available for collectors, and is often excellent value.

The fashion for jet started in the 1850s when Queen Victoria, in mourning for a cousin, wore a necklace of it to a banquet. Before long, jet, high-grade fossilized pine similar to a very hard coal or anthracite, was considered the only suitable material for full mourning; the jet brooch (*right*, Beauty & the Beasts, London) from the 1880s is polished to a deep shine. Whitby, a sleepy coastal town in Yorkshire, England, and the site of large jet deposits, had hitherto hardly been on the map. The town now became a busy industrial center, with the local jet being carved, turned, faceted, and polished by local craftsmen until it gleamed. Trade flourished, the shops filled with large black mourning jewels for sale to the throngs of jet hunters that visited the town. The death of Prince Albert in 1861 only added to Whitby's prosperity. By the end of the 19th century, imitations of jet were being made in costume jewelry

centers such as Gablonz, Bohemia, out of vulcanite, an early plastic which lacked the luster of the real thing, and out of shiny black glass. This "French" jet, as the glass simulation was known, became extremely popular, as it was hard enough to be cut into many facets and was highly reflective. Most French jet was backed with a black-coated steel and then glued, fused, or soldered onto a metal base to increase its sparkle. It can be hard to distinguish from real jet, although, like other paste jewels, it is cooler to the touch and sometimes contains air bubbles.

Although jet, along with other mourning jewels, was not used after the 1890s as an expression of grief, its deep, lustrous black coloring remained fashionable until the 1920s.

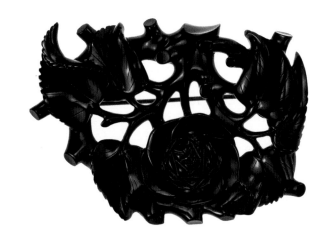

in mourning jewelry grew up in Britain, encouraged by the well-established practice of leaving a specific legacy for such pieces. Black mourning jewels of all kinds were contrived out of materials such as enamel, onyx, glass, Berlin cast iron, papier-maché, vulcanite, petrified oak from Irish bogs, and, above all, jet. Some mass-produced items had a compartment to hold a lock of the dead person's hair.

Human hair was not only used in mourning jewelry. From the earliest years of the new century, hairwork was created, incorporating lengths of braided human hair into decorative jewels. It remained resolutely unfashionable until the 1840s, when it suddenly enjoyed the sort of intense vogue that was typical of the era. It was worn everywhere, as watch chains, necklaces, bracelets, pendants, crosses, and earrings, woven and glued into place and mounted in gold or pinchbeck. Firms in both Paris and London strove to outdo each other with their *fantaisies diverses en cheveux* (diverse fantasies in hairwork); the leading French names were Lemonnier and Charleux, and Forrer in England. Hairwork is a good collecting area, as it has traditionally been spurned as somehow distasteful. Much of the workmanship used to incorporate hair into even, three-dimensional beadwork is of the highest quality, as are the mounts. Early examples are particularly highly sought, as later pieces were more often than not made out of coarse horsehair.

Whimsical Styles of the Late Century

The extraordinary upheavals and changes experienced throughout the century were expressed in a quest for endless novelties. The macabre was highly fashionable during the mid- and late 19th century, with women falling over themselves to wear the most gruesome of ornaments. Organic matter found its way into jewelry, from bone, coral, ivory, and tortoiseshell to the teeth and claws of tigers, and, most extreme of all, entire stuffed hummingbirds mounted on pins. These can fetch considerable sums today for their curiosity value. There was a fad for jewels that incorporated the sea snail's operculum, the knobbly, creamy or greenish "eye," set in gold or gilt metal, while shells of all types were collected by leisured women and strung on lengths of pretty ribbon as necklaces and other jewels. Today, such items in good, original condition are being collected for the first time, as reserves of most other types of 19th-century jewelry are beginning to dry up.

Despite a welter of new materials and influences, gold continued to be prized above all other metals in jewelry design, and was continually imitated by base metals. Between the 1860s and 1880s, Abyssinian gold, a brightly colored alloy, was incorporated into all forms of jewelry, while gilt metal was fashioned into a range of bangles, some set with a single large paste stone, others enameled or embossed. Gilt metal, like the lower (and therefore cheaper) carats of gold introduced earlier in the century, was also used for earrings, some of which were highly eccentric. The insect craze of the 1860s expanded into earrings in the form of bird's nests, trains, hats, and even willow-patterned plates, reflecting the interest in all things Oriental that sprang up after Japanese wares were shown at the second London International Exhibition in 1862. The first had been held the year before, and was the first time that exhibitors from other countries were invited to Britain.

Within the span of a hundred years, the established European social order had undergone far-reaching changes, with increased wealth for the general population and the arrival of the Machine Age. These developments, as we have seen, had been mirrored in costume jewelry design. But despite the apparent solidity of the era, there were more changes to come, as modern materials such as plastics came to the fore and couture design changed the face of fashion.

ALUMINUM JEWELRY APPEARS

■ At the Great Exhibition of 1851 held in Hyde Park, London, the first pieces of aluminum jewelry were displayed by their British maker. Aluminum was then rare and more expensive than gold. Although it was not a great success as jewelry material, since buyers found it too light for the relative cost, by the 1880s it was being sold as brooches and necklaces, stamped with designs or twisted into the ubiquitous branch and bar brooches. This necklace, box, and compact made around 1860 show how finely the new metal could be worked. Madeline Popper, London.

CHAPTER THREE

Garlands & Pearls

With the close of the 19th century, fashion became polarized between two distinct styles. Respectability vied with comfort in fashionable attire, and mass-produced costume jewelry was challenged by an artistic movement which championed the work of craftsmen. This short period, from the end of the 19th century and into the dawn of the new century, was an age of innocence before the dramatic upheaval and change which came after World War I.

THE AGE OF INNOCENCE

Before the storm of World War I, much of fashionable Europe was caught between the desire for respectability and the status quo, and the wish to move toward the sensuality of Art Nouveau.

Two utterly contrasting styles vied for attention at the end of the 19th century. While a minority of particularly style-conscious Europeans were caught up by the flowing line of Art Nouveau, radically different from anything that had appeared before, most of society remained unaffected. The women of the time were well aware of the new movement — a magazine illustration of the latest walking outfit might be surrounded with an Art Nouveau border, for example — but most tended to regard the comfortable silk and velvet "esthetic" day dresses, designed and manufactured for firms such as Liberty, as vulgar. They preferred to stick to the current interpretations of traditional styles, which exaggerated the feminine shape.

The Belle Epoque
"Respectable" women of the Belle Epoque, as the period between 1890 and 1910 was known in France, were clothed from neck to toe in elaborate, high-necked gowns which accentuated the fashionable S-shape. This restrictive style exaggerated the hips and pushed the chest forward into a mono-bosom, which was often padded to give the top-heavy look then considered essential. A body-compressing corset was used to achieve the shape, even though it was known to render its wearer infirm by distorting the spine and squashing the stomach and abdomen.

Such dress clearly signaled that the wearer was a wealthy and leisured woman who had no need for the practical, durable skirt and blouse worn by the working classes. On the contrary, those with time on their hands in the

Long drop earrings such as these of highly decorative paste (*top left*) enjoyed a revival around 1900, when women began to wear their hair up again. Trevor Allen, London. A large paste and gilt cuff bracelet made for Sarah Bernhardt (*top right*). Brixton Brady, London The eye of this dramatic early 1900s paste peacock brooch is highlighted by a single red stone (*bottom left*). Pastes and pearls are worked into fashionable garlands and bows on this 1910 pendant brooch (*bottom right*). Beauty & the Beasts, London.

Tiaras continued to be favored by society women well into the 20th century. This elegant example imitates the folds and fall of a ribbon, its white pastes set above a rail of silver. Trevor Allen, London.

Sarah Bernhardt's long career in the theater and her enormous popularity made her a very influencial figure in the world of costume jewelry. Many of the best designers in France vied to create jewelry for her, in the expectation that what she wore would soon become popular with the general public. Many of the pieces she commissioned were created specifically to wear on stage.

earliest years of the 20th century filled their leisure by constantly changing their clothes throughout the day. There were separate outfits for riding, motoring, golf, lunches, tea parties, garden parties, and balls; both men and women had a complete change of wardrobe for town and country. The cost of living was low, and a young man could enjoy himself to the full on a slender income; it was not his concern that the homeworkers making his white flannel shirts, each of which took an hour or more to finish, were paid a pittance.

The Purity of White

In the early part of the new century, women were especially taken with ultra-feminine, lacy dresses in impractical shades of white and pale, soft tones. This was in direct contrast to the strong colors and shapes of Art Nouveau. The suffragette movement was gathering momentum, and some women were keen to take a more active role in life than hitherto, but many others were anxious not to upset the status quo. The fashionable ruffles and flounces underlined this reluctance to discard a woman's traditional role as a pampered clothes-horse displaying a husband's wealth.

The preference for light shades brought in its train a revival of interest in diamonds and pearls. Newly opened diamond mines in South Africa meant that there was a ready supply of stones for the very wealthy, and jewelers experimented with different ways of setting them in the appropriately light-colored platinum, of all metals the most resistant to knocks and damage.

Platinum had been available since the mid-19th century, but it was difficult and dangerous to work. It had a very high melting point, and in the early years was mixed with mercuric oxide, a substance lethal enough to kill many of those who handled it. As a result, platinum was unpopular with jewelers until a safer method of working it was found at the turn of the century. It was heavy, but its silvery color and malleability (ability to be beaten very thin) made it an ideal setting for diamonds. Renowned Parisian jewelers such as Cartier, Boucheron, and the classic jewelers of the Place Vendôme and the Rue de la Paix turned out wonderful diamond and platinum tiaras, necklaces, earrings, and brooches. Their delicate, flowery designs looked back to the 18th-century rococo style popular in pre-Revolutionary France. Classical themes were employed in abundance on brooches and earrings, from drapes and swags to wreaths and garlands of flowers. Bows swept back into fashion as an essential accessory to be pinned to every available area of dress.

Diamonds were rarely combined with paste stones, although paste would be used to replace a diamond that had been lost. But in many cases, genuine diamonds were combined with synthetic stones, real gems "grown" in a laboratory. The scientists of the time were very proud of discovering this

Classical decorative motifs such as baskets and flowers enjoyed a revival during the ultra-feminine early years of the 20th century. This delicate flower basket necklace of pastes is linked to its decorative chain by the ubiquitous bow. Beauty & the Beasts, London.

process, and such synthetics were used in high-quality pieces. The best, especially faux emeralds, were hard to distinguish from true stones, but most had a brighter glow than natural gems. Today, such pieces are collectible for their novelty value, but are hard to come by, as often the synthetic stones were replaced with real gems by dealers keen to get the best price for a piece.

The delicate work on many of these pieces was easily matched by the superb workmanship found in the most costly bijouterie imitation, or fake jewelry. First-class examples of colorless paste were mounted in silver or white alloy copies of platinum, often in designs very similar to diamond pieces. Boucheron, for example, celebrated the first attempts at flight with his imaginative winged hair ornaments set with diamonds; these established a vogue for such jewels, produced in a variety of different materials and styles, that lasted until well after World War I. Today, such paste pieces are still available to collectors, with popular, practical styles, such as bow brooches, fetching the highest prices as long as they are in good condition. Real platinum pieces are rarely marked as such, but platinum is quite heavy and alloy copies are generally lighter in weight.

The Superiority of French Paste

The finest paste aspired to the same brilliance as true gems. As in earlier centuries, it was often no less carefully worked than real diamonds. The best was in demand by high-class jewelers all over the world, and one maker was universally acknowledged to provide the highest and most consistent quality: Daniel Swarovski. Parisian jewelers were major clients of Swarovski's. French paste was universally acknowledged as being of the highest standard, just as it had always been. The reputation of French paste workers, established by Stras and his contemporaries, was continued throughout the time of the Belle Epoque by firms such as Besson, Alexandre Royé, Galand, and Madame Navez. Their paste pieces ranged

The white pastes of this delicate, feminine bracelet from the early 1900s are set in silver. Wide bracelets such as this were very popular, sometimes worn over the top of long, tight sleeves or gloves. Trevor Allen, London.

Princess Alexandra helped
popularize sautoirs such as this
Lalique-inspired example. It would
be worn over a high-necked dress.
Tessa Innes, England

from spectacular settings of imitation diamonds to smaller jewels that epitomized the taste for genteel femininity and incorporated quiet colors, from aquamarine and soft pink, to dusty cinnamons and greens. Garlands and swags were still very much in vogue.

Most paste was set in mounts of silver, an obvious substitute for platinum, although it could not be worked so finely. Silver settings are therefore generally slightly thicker than platinum ones, although much of the workmanship is still very good. French paste of the period is fairly hard to come by, and can vary in condition, but a number of pendants and brooches can still be picked up for affordable sums.

Suffragette Jewelry

Much distinctive jewelry was made for the British suffragette movement during this period; wearing it was a quiet way of showing support for the movement. Its trademark colors of green, violet, and white stood for "Give Votes to Women." It could easily have been taken to show royalist fervor, as mauve was said to be Alexandra's favorite color, while the leek-green peridot was the Prince of Wales's jewel of choice. As a result, quantities of fashionable paste incorporated these colors. It is an area that has only recently begun to be collected, and so some unexpected bargains can still turn up, with paste examples fetching a wide range of prices. The three colors were incorporated into jewelry of all types, especially brooches and pendants, but a specifically suffragette piece will sell for roughly double the price of a purely decorative piece inspired by royal taste, of the same date.

Pearl Appeal

At King Edward VII's coronation in 1901, Queen Alexandra's jewelry dazzled onlookers. Her neck was encircled with no less than five diamond chokers, while seven strings of magnificent pearls, measuring 2 ft (65 cm) or more in length, hung down over a splendid corsage ornament of yet more diamonds and creamy pearls. There followed a swift change in taste as Alexandra's attachment to pearls, already reflected in imitations, was adopted by fashionable society. Diamonds were still fine for formal wear, but pearls strung into necklaces and wound around the neck became essential accessories for socialites and aristocrats right up to the 1920s.

This was not the first time that pearls had been the height of fashion. They had been incorporated into jewelry of all types for thousands of years, above all by the ancient Romans and again in the 16th century. Now they were once more in the ascendant, taking on the significance that diamonds had had for recent generations, their number and size a benchmark of their wearer's status and wealth. The most prized pearls were those of a good, bright white with few, if any, blemishes, although pearls with a slight cream, pink, or gray tint were also valued, especially as they matched the favored dress colors of the time.

Queen Alexandra's fondness for the *collier de chien* (dog collar) made these close-fitting pearl chokers especially desirable. Several single-strand chokers might be worn together, or a deep dog-collar of several rows would be worn alone, wrapping the neck in pearls from jawline to collarbone. Some chokers were made of tiny seed pearls. Equally popular and even more impressive were pearl *sautoirs* (long necklaces), worn over a high-collared dress or wound around the throat and then falling to the bustline or below. Such necklaces would be accompanied by pearl earrings dangling from ears exposed by upswept hairstyles.

Pearls and diamonds were frequently combined on corsage ornaments, on chokers, on tiaras, and in necklaces. Only the wealthiest could afford real diamonds and pearls, but, just as the paste trade had developed 200 years earlier to provide the less well-off with a fashionable alternative, so too did the trade in imitation pearls flourish at the turn of the century. Before long,

The Influence of Alexandra

■ In Britain, the vogue for diamonds and pearls was greatly accentuated by the taste and style of the Danish-born Princess of Wales, later Queen Alexandra (1844–1925), admired for her elegance and beauty. A woman of simple tastes, her royal duties demanded the wearing of formal jewels: tiaras and impressive necklaces of diamonds, pearls, and amethysts. She was particularly fond of hair ornaments of all types: the aigrette enjoyed a revival at this time, thanks to her. Alexandra also initiated the fad for narrow pearl chokers and the more substantial *collier de chien*, or dog-collar, in which several rows of pearls were strung together to form a deep choker. She is thought to have favored them as they emphasized her long neck and concealed an unsightly birthmark.

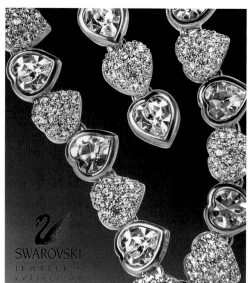

SWAROVSKI
JEWELER'S
collection

Daniel Swarovski, Stonemaker Extraordinaire

■ Daniel Swarovski was born in 1862 in Georgenthal, a small village in the Iser Mountains of Bohemia. The eldest son, he grew up learning the trade of his father, a gemcutter. In Vienna he visited an international design and technology exhibition that made a lasting impression on him. After working briefly in Paris, he joined his father's business. There he constantly experimented with ways of cutting the glass stones that he and his father, and later his father-in-law, produced. Eventually he came up with a method of producing small, "brilliant-cut" crystal stones of such high quality that the firm received numerous orders from Paris, London, and the United States. But the paste business was a competitive one, and hand-cutting the glass stones was labor intensive. In order to meet deadlines and cut costs, Swarovski turned his attention to inventing a mechanical stone-cutter, to shape and facet numerous stones simultaneously without losing any

of the firm's much-vaunted quality. It took a while to find the solution, but in 1891 Swarovski took out a patent for his mechanical "comb," which was able to produce great numbers of high-quality ornamental stones at great speed. His invention could not have come at a better moment, coinciding as it did with the renewed craze for diamonds and cut gems. The workmanship in his glass gems was recognized by jewelers and their clientéle alike, and large amounts were exported to fashionable centers in Europe and farther afield.

So successful did the firm become that, in 1895, Swarovski decided to move it away from the prying eyes of competitors, and founded a cutting plant in the rural backwater of Wattens, in western Austria. He continued to import raw materials from Bohemia, churning out quantities of his Tyrolean Cut Stones, as they became known. The firm has maintained its reputation for top-quality glass stones ever since, and still provides them for the costume jewelry trade today.

TRUE OR FALSE?

■ The best way of determining whether a pearl is an imitation or not is to rub it against your teeth. Natural pearls harvested from the wild have a slightly gritty texture, as the pearl has growth rings a little like those found in the trunk of a tree. Imitation pearls are mostly made from glass and have a completely smooth surface.

jewelers were providing an eager public with all kinds of imitation paste and pearl pieces. Dog-collars were made in quantity, the "pearls" threaded onto wire instead of the more usual strings of silk, the rigid side-bars set with paste rather than diamonds. Collectors can still pick up such items, although in many cases the imitation pearls have not stood the test of time particularly well, and often show yellowing or other signs of age. As usual, the better the condition of the piece, the higher the price it will command.

The Art of Imitating Pearls

By 1908, pearls were considered indispensable by the well-to-do, as important as their houses, horses, and cars. Inevitably, the ever-growing middle classes strained to keep up with the leaders of polite society, and it was not long before very good imitation pearls were being made all over the world. Some of the best came out of the workshops of French firms such as Tècla, Suclier, and Richelieu, and these were renowned as "Paris pearls."

Fake pearls had in fact been in production for centuries, both in Europe and farther afield. The Romans had a technique for making them, as did Native Americans. The earliest known French imitation pearls date back to the 16th century, when in 1565 a rosary-maker named Joaquin stumbled on a technique for coating beads with a pearl-like substance. He had just finished washing some freshly caught fish when he accidentally dropped a set of beads into the basin of water in which he was rinsing the fish, and was amazed to see that they took on the appearance of pearls. What Joaquin discovered was that fish scales contain a pearl-like iridescence, and he was able to extract it. The resulting liquid was strained and purified before being added to a lacquer or similar substance to make a paste. This thick paste was applied to solid or hollow beads, which would need up to ten coats for an adequately lustrous look. In most cases the beads were sprayed or dipped. This later became known as *essence d'orient*, or pearl essence, and was widely used in the early 20th century as a coating for glass or plastic wax-filled beads which were then sold as imitation pearls. Pearl essence was made in France right up to 1939. It was widely used by firms such as Canvet of Paris, a company known for its *perles métalliques*, which had a distinctive metallic finish.

Cultured Pearls

Cultured pearls are far more common than natural ones. They were being produced by the end of the 19th century, and by about 1915, the Japanese had totally mastered the art of cultivating them. The pearls are encouraged to grow by inserting a small mother-of-pearl bead into an oyster, which then surrounds it with a pearl coating. Top-quality cultured pearls are hard to tell from natural ones, although it is sometimes possible to see the mother-of-pearl bead from the drill hole. The widespread production of the cultured pearl completely undermined the value of real ones, and today, small natural pearls fetch far less than they used to. Cultured pearls, on the other hand, are still extremely popular; a good secondhand string costs as little as an eighth of the price of a new one.

Pearls had little part to play in the jewelry inspired by the new artistic movement which burst into life in the mid-1890s, and which made a strong contrast with the garlands and bows beloved of middle-class society. Different manifestations of Art Nouveau were to blossom in the next two decades in France (where it was called *Le style moderne*), Germany (*Jugendstil*), Austria (*Sezession style*), Italy (*Stile Liberty*), and in Scotland.

A fascination with Darwin's ideas on evolution led to a spate of monkey brooches in the late 19th and early 20th centuries. In this example the monkeys are set with white paste, although their eyes are featured in red. They are linked to each other by a fine gold chain. Trevor Allen, London.

Long hairstyles for women meant that haircombs were always needed. Combs were an early candidate for mass production, especially those made in the first plastics, such as this pale yellow ivorine comb. Trevor Allen, London.

CHAPTER FOUR

The Sinuous Line

At the turn of the century, while most grand society ladies in Britain and America were lacing themselves into restrictive corsets and tight bodices, mainland Europe was alive with the sense of a new era. The *fin-de-siècle* abandon and spirit of sexual freedom that was taking hold in Paris and neighboring capitals found expression in the swirling, sensual lines of Art Nouveau, literally, New Art. Although in general, it was adopted by only the most avant-garde sections of society, this innovative style percolated through the Arts and Crafts movement in northern Europe and gave a kick start to America's burgeoning costume jewelry industry.

PURE ART NOUVEAU

The new movement left a lasting impression on architecture, interior design, furniture, glass and ceramics, posters, advertising, and jewelry. The explosion of industrial mass production brought these innovative products within the range of a widely expanded market.

The new approach to art and design originated in the intellectual hotbed of late 19th-century Paris. It took its name from an art gallery, *La Maison de l'Art Nouveau*, set up in 1895 by Siegfried Bing, a dealer in Japanese art, as an outlet for the most exciting work by the young designers of the day: jewelers, glassmakers, potters, and fabric designers. Much of their output employed the flowing curves and twisting shapes that exemplified the new style. Within five years, by the time of the 1900 Paris *Exposition des Arts Universelles*, Art Nouveau was an internationally recognized design movement that surfaced in architecture and all the decorative arts throughout Europe.

Graphic designers, metalworkers, interior designers, and furniture makers joined the ranks of artists who were affected by the new style. Inexpensive trinkets and ornaments, mass-produced, stamped from sheets of silver or gilt metal, but beautifully designed, allowed even the lowest-paid store clerk to feel part of a modern age. Nowhere were the ideals of the Art Nouveau movement more succinctly expressed than in the jewelry of the time, which was sold in quantity in new department stores opening all over the world. The finest pieces incorporated the primary Art Nouveau motifs of natural forms and an androgynous face or head into ornaments that the modern woman could wear without breaking the bank.

A Frances McNair silver and enamel brooch (*top left*), 1900. Peacock feather buckle of enamel and glass on metal (*top right*) by Piel Frères, 1900. The peacock theme is continued by C. R. Ashbee's silver gilt, abalone, and enamel pendant (*bottom left*) dated 1907. The same designer produced the silver, enamel, and turquoise drop brooch (*bottom right*), 1900. Tadema Gallery, London.

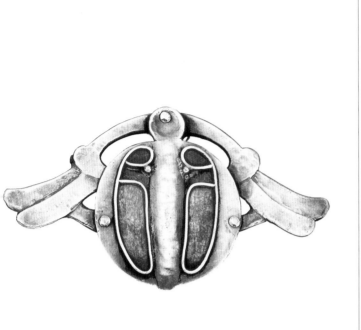

This carved horn comb set with sapphires and dated around 1900, is attributed to Lucien Gaillard and signed Kozan in Japanese script. It is accompanied by its original box. Tadema Gallery, London.

Jewels as Art

A great deal of jewelry was sold in Paris galleries in the 1890s. It is interesting that the German art critic Julius Meier Graefe set up his own establishment, *La Maison Moderne*, in Paris at around this time. Much "art" jewelry consisted of one-off pieces by such designers as Paul Follot, Maurice Dufrêne, Théodore Lambert, and René Lalique. These designers were to become the leading lights of Art Nouveau, and jewelry by such makers is now out of reach of all but the wealthiest collectors; most of it is tucked away in private collections or on display in public museums. But their ideas were seminal, opening the way for others to follow them.

Throughout Europe, jewelers experimented with combining precious and non-precious materials in bold, original designs, and explored the commercial possibilities of mass production. For the first time in history, "art" jewels of superb design and workmanship could be made cheaply and in quantity, to be sold to a wide spectrum of the population. The trend for wearing imitation jewels, which started with 18th-century paste and accelerated during the Industrial Revolution of the mid-19th century, was poised to take the 20th century by storm, as manufacturers flooded the market with inexpensive designer jewels, the precursors of true costume jewelry of the 1920s to 1950s.

The glassmaker and jeweler René Lalique and his colleague Lucien Gaillard were fascinated by horn, a malleable, translucent material rarely used in the West except in hair combs, but popular in Japan. In the 1890s Lalique produced a line of horn combs set with stones, while Gaillard specialized in horn jewelry, carving and then coating it. His techniques were

The Mastery of Lalique

■ Perhaps best known today for his glass, the Frenchman René Lalique (1860–1945) was also a consummate jeweler, and possibly the finest goldsmith of the Art Nouveau period (the Egyptian ring above in gold, enamel, and opal is a rare example of his talent.) His jewelry was astonishingly imaginative and bold, his designs combining precious stones and metals with intrinsically worthless materials, such as glass, horn, and steel, in a way that finally broke with all previous conventions.

He drew inspiration from countless sources, ranging from Japanese design, whose clean lines, symmetry, mixed materials, and use of color were enormously influential, to Sarah Bernhardt, an actress whose eccentric, extravagant ideas and

enthusiasms were a catalyst for some of Lalique's most extraordinary jewels. His rings, bracelets, brooches, necklaces, and tiaras were famous in his own lifetime, recognized as works of art and exhibited to critical acclaim throughout Europe and beyond. Many of his jewels were considered bizarre, even shocking, but with them Lalique established a new age of imaginative jewelry, in which craftsmen felt free to copy his uninhibited approach to both form and materials.

Although jewelry crafted by Lalique himself is now extremely rare and expensive to buy, his company made a wide range of jewels, some of which were reasonably priced at the time, and can still be found today. Molded glass pendants and stick pins appear in sales from time to time, fetching prices within the range of most collectors, while Lalique-inspired pieces manufactured by companies such as Maison Gripoix, especially if they are signed, are worth looking out for. A fair number of such pieces were relatively poorly manufactured, however, and are not in particularly good condition today.

Dating from 1900, this Jugendstil silver gilt, garnet, and chalcedony pendant was designed by Eduard Schopflich.
Tadema Gallery, London.

A common motif running through much of Art Nouveau is a woman's head with flowing hair. This motif is used here on a silver, ivory, and abalone brooch made by Theodor Schmidt in 1900.
Tadema Gallery, London.

later widely imitated on mid-priced pendants and brooches, especially by the young French designers Elisabeth Bonté, a graduate of the *Ecole des Arts Décoratifs* (School of Decorative Arts) in Paris, and Georges Pierre, who signed himself GIP. These two pooled their design talents to produce a selection of pendants, all signed, until 1936, by which time the availability of plastic made horn a redundant material. They are still collectible today. Plain, signed horn pendants are fairly affordable; more interesting pieces, in the shape of an insect or butterfly, will sell for twice as much.

The Cult of Woman

The Art Nouveau movement greatly appealed to women. Its free-flowing, naturalistic curves had a sleek, sophisticated softness that chimed with women's aspirations for emancipation. Flamboyant role models such as the actress Sarah Bernhardt (1844–1923) were seen to embrace their sexuality rather than hide it under tight corsets and high-necked dresses, and images of women in loose, flowing robes, created by graphic artists such as the Czech-born Alphonse Mucha, started to appear in Europe. Mucha (1860–1939), who did much to promote the Art Nouveau movement, made his name by designing publicity posters for Bernhardt's plays.

As Bernhardt's reputation grew, leading jewelers lined up for a chance to adorn her with their creations. Her influence on jewelry design and tastes was extensive, and low-priced copies of her legendary ornaments, produced by firms such as Maison Gripoix and Bijoux Bardach, sold in fashionable boutiques all over Paris. Made of metal and paste, and often decorated with enamel, these popular theatrical accessories were sold in their thousands and can still be found today, although many are too battered to warrant collection.Bernhardt's fame mirrored the turn-of-the-century obsession with the female form, both in design and in the fine art and literature of the time.

THE FACE MOTIF

■ Countless small costume jewelry firms in the
United States turned out pieces that featured the
female face, and "Gibson Girl" brooches were
common, the distinctive, youthful profile
surrounded by abundant locks of hair. In the
example above, the hair flows into and becomes
the silver gilt petals in the 1900 brooch (Tadema
Gallery, London.) In 1903, the firm of Averbeck &
Averbeck produced a line of buckles typifying this
trend, in which a female face with flowing hair
formed the centerpiece. The design was known as
Flor-a-Dora, named after a musical comedy
which was playing to packed houses in both
London and New York.

A female face, surrounded by long, flowing hair, appeared on all kinds of Art
Nouveau objects, particularly on jewelry. Even though Art Nouveau in its
most sensual form was thought to be in questionable taste in the more
conservative homes of Britain and the United States, where corseted
respectability reigned supreme, the face motif occurred again and again in
jewelry design.

American Costume Jewelers

In the United States, the popularity of the female motif was partly due to the
ubiquitous "Gibson Girl," the creation of an American illustrator, Charles
Dana Gibson (1867–1944), who drew her for magazines such as *Collier's* and
Life. This fictional character encapsulated all the female qualities that were
held to be desirable between the 1890s and 1914, and went a long way to
encourage the emancipation of American womanhood.

The female face was the focus of much of the jewelry turned out by the
Unger Brothers, based in New Jersey, who started to produce inexpensive
items from 1878 on. Over the next ten years, Philomen Dickinson, the firm's
chief designer, produced endless variations on plant and face motifs, much in
silver and gilt metal, and some set with semiprecious stones. Even if the
French Art Nouveau style was not adopted in its most extreme form in the
United States, Dickinson, like many American designers, was much
influenced by the Paris Exposition of 1900.

Tiffany Takes Up Art Nouveau

Art Nouveau design motifs appeared in the output of numerous firms, both
large and small, including that of America's leading jewelers, Tiffany & Co.
Tiffany had been producing jewelry since the early 19th century, and had two

main production centers, in Newark, New Jersey, and in Providence, Rhode Island. Although the company was founded in 1834, it was under the direction of Louis Comfort Tiffany (1848–1933), the founder's son, that it first began to make a name for itself as one of the world's leading jewelers. Tiffany, like Lalique in France, was a famous glassmaker who turned his hand to jewelry, combining precious and non-precious materials as Lalique did, albeit in a very different fashion; his designs were as much influenced by the crafts revival in Britain at the time, as they were by Art Nouveau.

In 1902, the firm opened an art jewelry department in its New York shop, selling a select line of top-of-the-market pieces designed by Tiffany himself. Although the department had a short life — it closed in 1916 — and dealt in art, rather than costume, jewelry, Tiffany's jewels had as much impact on the western side of the Atlantic as Lalique's pieces had in Europe. Young designers exposed to Tiffany's ideas went on to produce distinctly American jewelry, combining precious and non-precious materials, which helped to establish Providence as the center of the American costume jewelry industry.

Today, any 19th- and early 20th-century artifacts produced by Tiffany are seized by collectors, with the very best pieces snapped up by the firm itself for its own archives. Handcrafted pieces by Tiffany himself are almost impossible to come by, but, as with Lalique, the company did produce and sell cheaper imitations of their top-flight jewels, and these can still be found.

Another American firm based in Providence was the Gorham Corporation, founded in the early 19th century. Gorham had employed a number of English jewelry designers from its foundation, and from around 1890 it built on its success by producing a line of Gallic-influenced jewelry trademarked Martelé. Farther south, in Newark, New Jersey, the firm of William B. Kerr & Co. was also producing Art Nouveau costume jewelry. Originally known as Kerr & Thierry when it was founded in 1855 to make tableware and gold and silver jewelry, between 1892 and 1900 the firm was producing large quantities of hollow-backed jewels stamped with imitation repoussé work, most of it based on French Art Nouveau designs and marked with a French-style fleur-de-lys.

A silver and enamel pendant titled "Sanctuary" and dated 1902, was designed by architect Robert Lorimer. Tadema Gallery, London.

TRADITIONAL ARTS AND CRAFTS

The Arts and Crafts movement in Britain found sympathetic followers in other northern European countries and influenced craftsmen and artists working in Germany and Austria.

Although the curving forms of French Art Nouveau did find their way into some British design, the movement did not take hold in Britain as it had elsewhere. A prudishness left over from the previous age spurned its overt sensuality, and tastes turned instead to the more restrained Arts and Crafts movement. This began essentially as a reaction to the Machine Age, led by the British art critic John Ruskin (1819–1900) and his fellow spirit William Morris. They and others urged a return to pre-industrial levels of craftsmanship, looking back to the Middle Ages and beyond for inspiration, and a number of designers in Britain and elsewhere responded to their ideas.

Furniture makers, architects, and interior designers were drawn to the movement along with jewelers, most of whom produced costly one-off pieces with superb workmanship, spurning the material benefits that came with mass production. But although the time and effort expended on these pieces meant that they were too expensive to be thought of as costume jewelry, the

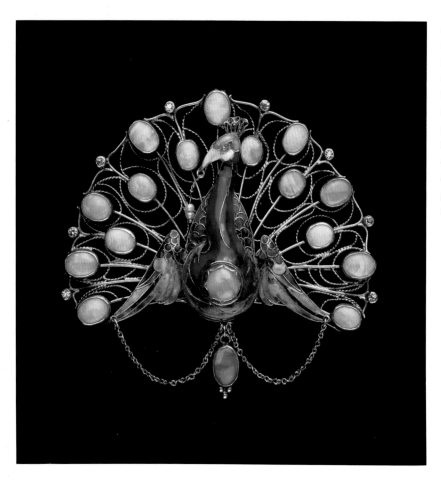

A series of Jugendstil brooches (*opposite page*) date from 1900. (*Clockwise, from the top*): silver and green chalcedony brooch by Fahrner; silver, enamel, and amethyst brooch by Fahrner; silver gilt, chalcedony, and pearl brooch by Levinger and Hissinger; silver, coral, and pearl brooch; gold, pearl, and ruby brooch; gold, opal, and pearl brooch (*center*) all by Murrle Bennett. Tadema Gallery, London.

A British Arts and Crafts peacock brooch in silver, enamel, opals, and diamonds (*above*) dating from 1905. Tadema Gallery, London.

socialist principles behind the movement encouraged its followers to explore the design potential of cheap materials as well as precious ones. Certain designers did not stick rigidly to the principles of the movement, and were not averse to marrying fine design with industrial techniques of production. The stock sold by the entrepreneur and shopkeeper A.L. Liberty was the most famous result. It could not by rights be thought of as pure Arts and Crafts, but in concept it was deeply indebted to the British movement.

Liberty launched the Celtic revival, bringing it to the notice of the British public, and subsequently the rest of the world, with his Cymric line of jewelry. So successful was it that imitators soon sprang up. Among the best known, and collectible, pieces are those by Murrle, Bennett & Co., a London wholesaler who marketed close imitations of Liberty brooches and pendants that were actually mass-produced in limited runs by, among others, the Pforzheim company Theodor Fahrner.

But Liberty's team were not the only talented jewelry designers in Britain. Kate Harris designed a line of jewels for the silversmith William Hutton & Sons, while Charles Horner of Halifax specialized in mass-produced silver jewelry, particularly hat pins, between 1905–1914. Charles Horner, Sr., a pioneer of mass production, built the firm a new factory in 1905 with the profits from his invention, the Dorcas thimble, and his son, Charles, expanded the jewelry side of the business. Great numbers of pendants, brooches, and hat pins were made, based on simplified Liberty designs and given a touch of color with enamel, often in a characteristic Art Nouveau shade of peacock blue. Most shimmered with swirling Art Nouveau forms, although a number sported the winged scarab. Today, Horner pieces are not too expensive. The plainer the piece, the lower the price, although this is an increasingly popular collecting area, so prices are beginning to rise.

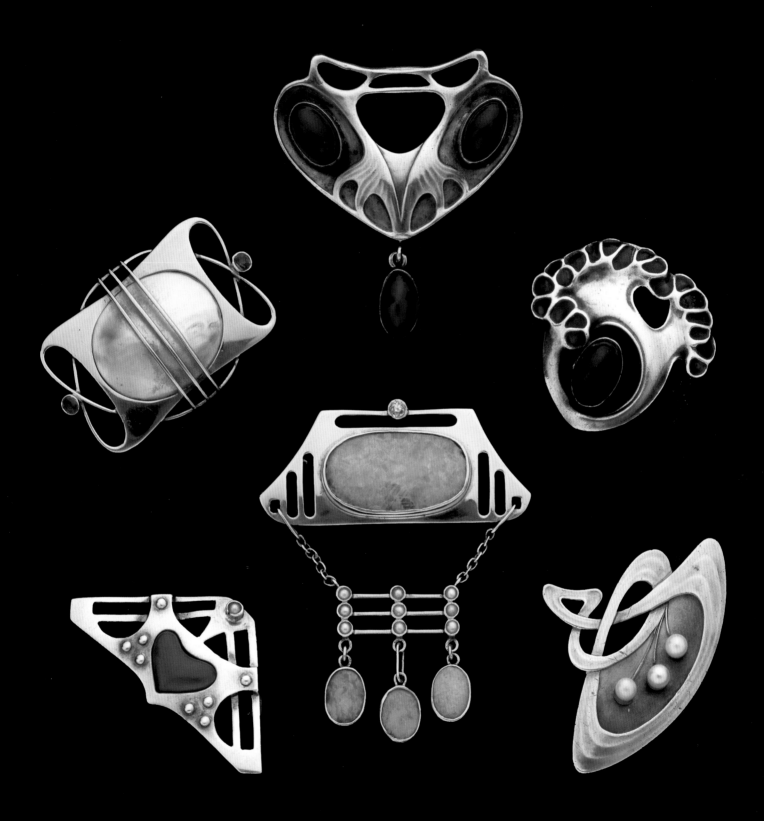

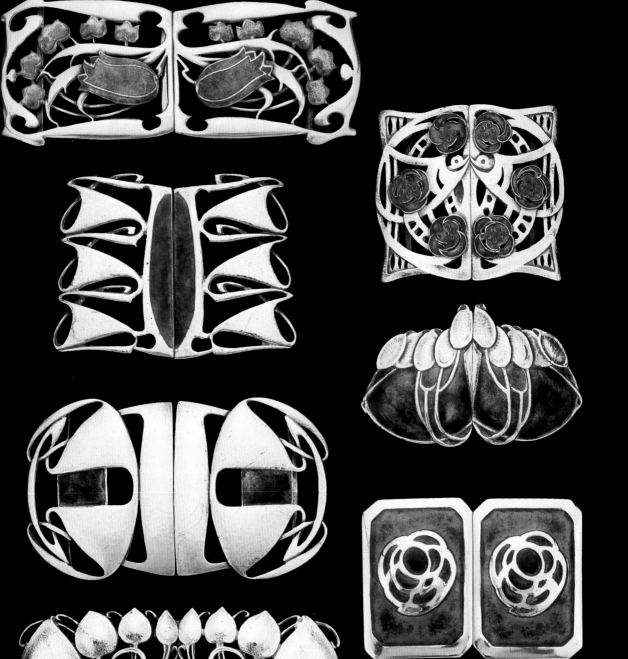

Jessie M. King silver and enamel buckle (*right*) and the buckles opposite designed for Liberty in 1900 display the revival of interest in Celtic motifs.
Tadema Gallery, London.

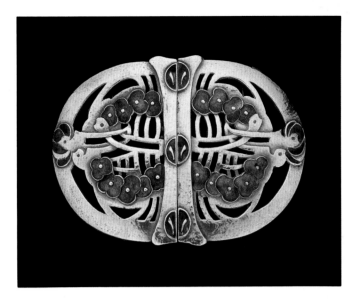

Liberty and the Celtic Revival

■ When Arthur Lasenby Liberty (1843–1917) first grasped the commercial possibilities of the Arts and Crafts movement, and the talent of some of its leading designers, he was working as a buyer in Oriental art and objects for a high-class London retailer. By 1875, he had opened his first store, East India House in Regent Street, and began to commission pieces of jewelry and furniture to sell, running contests with a leading art magazine of the time, *Studio*, to find the best new designers. From 1894 on, he encouraged a team of talented freelancers to produce designs for mass production, and by 1900 his store was selling a vast selection of European and Oriental wares. The jewelry included rings, necklaces, bracelets, brooches, buckles, and pendants of smooth or hammered silver or sometimes gold, decorated with enameling and semiprecious stones.

Two of the most important figures in his design team were Archibald Knox (1864–1953), a native of the Isle of Man (part of Britain's Celtic fringe) and a leading force behind the Arts and Crafts Celtic revival, and Jessie M. King (1875–1949), a member of the Glasgow School of artists, an illustrator and designer. It was Knox who designed Liberty's highly influential Cymric line of gold and silver jewelry, launched in the late 1890s, while King designed jewelry, fabrics, and wallpapers for Liberty from 1902. She specialized in enameled silver belt buckles whose shapes are reminiscent of geometric designs by the Glaswegian architect and designer Charles Rennie Mackintosh (1868–1928); they were produced in huge numbers.

Many of Knox's creations, such as the interlaced metal designs filled with blue and green enamel, were made in Birmingham by W. H. Haseler & Co. This firm was founded in 1870, and in 1901 went into partnership with Liberty & Co. to launch Liberty & Co. (Cymric) Ltd. Most of its products were inexpensive pieces marked L & C Cymric. They were made to look handcrafted by stamping the surface with hammer marks or adding touches of enamel.

Collectors of early Liberty pieces can still hope to find a good selection of marked silver brooches, necklaces, and pendants, many of which still have their original fitted boxes. In some cases, the box may be stamped Liberty while the piece itself is not, especially if the jewelry was made abroad for the company. A piece with its box commands two to three times the price of one without.

A group of waist clasps of silver and enamel, including some designed by Jessie M. King (*those on the right*) and Archibold Knox (*those on the left*) for Liberty in 1900. Tadema Gallery, London.

Silver and gold gem set Secessionist
pendant (*above*) executed by Oscar
Dietrich in 1910. The two Jugendstil
brooches of silver and enamel (*below*)
date from around 1900 and are very rare.
Tadema Gallery, London.

Germany and Austria

Although Arts and Crafts was essentially an English movement, it had some interesting links with Germany. One of Queen Victoria's daughters, Princess Alice, was married to the German Grand Duke Ernst-Ludwig of Hesse, and took many English ideas to the court at Darmstadt. Her husband admired some aspects of Arts and Crafts, such as allowing artists to work in freedom, unhindered by commercial pressures, and the fostering of traditional craftsmen's skills. He did not, however, share the original Arts and Crafts socialist ideals.

The Grand Duke set up an artists' colony at Mathildenhohe in 1899, where designers were free to explore their ideas. Although, in time, the colony came to be seen primarily as a propaganda exercise for Germany as a whole and for Hesse himself, a number of talented designers spent some time working there. The colony's first exhibition, in 1901, showcased the work of established designers such as Peter Behrens (1868–1940), Joseph Maria Olbrich (1867–1908) and Patriz Huber, among others, and had a recognizable influence on those whose significance was to come, such as Georg Kleemann.

In fact, the Darmstadt colony was more successful at promoting talent than the English Arts and Crafts, not least because it had closer connections

Theodor Fahrner,
Artistic Industrialist

■ The highly reputable firm of Theodor Fahrner had a pedigree in costume jewelry that stretched back to 1855, when Seeger & Fahrner first opened a factory in the German town of Pforzheim. The competition was formidable; by 1902, there were some 660 costume jewelry factories in the town, but nonetheless the company prospered.

By 1895, Fahrner had become the sole proprietor of the business and had moved his premises to 52 Luisenstrasse, where he sold small pieces of steel jewelry including rings, pins, and brooches. He presented his strikingly simple pieces at the Paris *Exposition Universelle* in 1900, winning a silver medal for his firm, despite the extreme contrast of his designs with those of the much fêted René Lalique. Although the two designers appeared to have little in common, they did share a belief that the artistic merit of a piece was more significant than the value of the materials used to make it.

The firm's trademark "TF" was registered in 1901, and a remarkable number of talented designers provided ideas for Fahrner to manufacture, from Kleemann and Huber to Ferdinand Morawe and Olbrich. Festoon necklaces of silver and enamel, set with amethysts, and decorated with chain tassels,

were typical of the work of Georg Kleemann, who was designing for Fahrner as early as 1902–3. Fahrner's pieces were exhibited and exported worldwide. By the time the *Fahrner Schmuck* (Fahrner Jewelry) line was introduced in 1910, the company was employing over 80 people. Despite various changes over the years, becoming Gustav Braendle, Theodor Fahrner Succ. in 1921, the firm remained in business until 1979. Early Fahrner pieces are very collectible, and expensive, as long as they are stamped with one of the wide range of marks the company used; without the stamp, the same, mass-produced piece is worth a fraction of the price.

An elaborate George Kleemann brooch (*left*) of gilded silver, *plique à jour*, turquoise, amethyst, garnet, and pearls is dated 1907. The silver and enamel brooch (*above*) was designed by Kolo Moser and made by Georg Scheidt in 1900. Tadema Gallery, London.

with top manufacturers. The need for industrial jewelry to be simple was emphasized, and close ties were established with the manufacturer Theodor Fahrner, who also had links with Murrle, Bennett & Co. As most of the German designers were not craftsmen, it was essential to find a producer they could trust, and Fahrner was considered the ultimate "artistic industrialist," one of the few that attempted to bridge the huge gap between art and industry.

The Austrian Movements

In Austria, too, concerned aristocrats were keen to keep traditional craftsmen in employment, in the face of the threat from the rise of industrialization. The Austrian Museum of Art and Industry was founded in 1867, and graduates of the Royal Arts and Crafts school, attached to the museum, formed the influential artistic cooperative of the Wiener Werkstätte, founded in 1903 by the designers Josef Hoffmann and Koloman Moser, and backed by the financier Fritz Warndorfer.

Hoffmann (1870–1956) and Moser (1868–1918) were founder members of the Vienna Sezession (Secession), a group of radical artists, set up in 1897, who had at first embraced the sinuous lines of French Art Nouveau, but gradually developed their own style. Geometric forms, symmetry, and contrasts of black and white, shadow and light, dominated Wiener Werkstätte design, percolating into furniture, glassware, pottery, metalwork, and stark, dramatic jewelry that was both formal and simple in feel. Few such pieces come up for sale today, but their designs foreshadowed the Machine-Age linearity of the Art Deco style that was to reign supreme in the 1920s.

Simply Modern

Most of the jewelry produced between World War I and World War II is described as Art Deco. This bold, geometric style was applied to architecture, furniture, ceramics, and even clothes, and advances in mass production and communication made it a truly international trend. Costume jewelry was one of Art Deco's clearest and most attractive expressions. It was unfussy, unfeminine, and unsentimental; cool and detached, unlike Art Nouveau, it shunned emotion and appealed to the eye and the intellect.

STYLE GOES INTERNATIONAL

Costume jewelry has always commented on and sometimes copied jewelry made with real gems and precious metals. "Fashion" jewelry was linked much more closely with fashionable clothes and became an important accessory just after World War I.

Women's fashion changed quite dramatically over a period of little more than ten years. Before World War I, the fashionable lady wore a whalebone corset that squeezed her body into an exaggerated hourglass shape, but this voluptuousness was then subverted by the qualities of her outer clothing: heavy, concealing fabrics in the quietest colors; long, trailing, complicated skirts; and lace-trimmed blouses buttoned up to the chin. She looked shy and demure under a silken parasol, or else was overwhelmed by a vast hat, and covered in fussy jewelry in the form of baskets, bows, and birds. The general effect was of an innocent, ingenuous girl in need of a gentleman's protection.

Fashionable young women of the 1920s wanted no part of this overly encumbered, submissive sensuality. Their modern, drop-waisted, *garçonne* (boyish) look was long, lean, and mean, described by the writer Aldous Huxley as "angular, flexible, and tubular like a section of a boa constrictor . . . dressed in clothes that emphasized this serpentine slimness." Only a minority of women had this natural body shape, so loose, straight-cut clothing provided the required outline and a new obsession with dieting, breast-binding, and girdles did the rest. Womanly curves were rejected in favor of a more boyish, linear silhouette. Short hair, bobbed, shingled, or cropped, completed the androgynous look. Ironically, the *garçonne* style combined its boyishness with the unprecedented exposure of large areas of

Early 1930s rhinestone floral brooch by Coro (*top left*). Steinberg & Tolkien, London. Carved Bakelite frog brooch on gilt metal, *c.* 1930 (*top right*) and a Bakelite dagger brooch (*bottom left*) from the same period. Christopher St. James, Ritzy, London. A late 1930s wheelbarrow fur clip of rhinestones and molded glass stones carved Cartier-style by Alfred Philippe for Trifari (*bottom right*). William Wain, London.

An early advertisement for Van Cleef & Arpels, the famed French jewelry house that produced the most magificent precious pieces. Their work was widely copied in paste and base metal by the costume jewelry industry. This sleeveless drop-waisted dress and long pearl rope epitomized the 1920s flapper look. Van Cleef & Arpels, Paris.

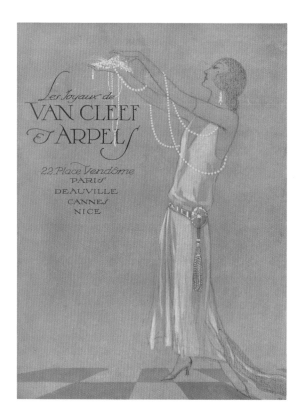

Art Deco necklace in diamonds and platinum by Van Cleef & Arpels, the firm that inspired decades of costume jewelry designers. Van Cleef & Arpels, Paris.

A modern basket brooch in Art Deco style by Jorge Cohen, made from original 1920s and 1930s crystals and pastes. Deco originals of this type are very scarce so good-quality reproductions have become popular and fetch high prices in their own right. Steven Miners, Cristobal, London.

the body. Hemlines fluctuated, then quickly settled on a point just below the knee, while dresses were often sleeveless and deeply cut at the front or back.

The new "undressed" androgyny represented far more than a mere fad in frocks. Women of all social classes were living a far more active, unrestricted, and varied life than their immediate predecessors, and it was the physical demands of this freedom that fueled the fashion revolution. The 1920s woman had driven trains during the war, she had worked in factories, on farms, and witnessed a whole generation of men being wiped off the face of the earth. From the aristocrat to the boy next door, everyone was affected by the war, the defining event of the early 20th century.

There was simply no way back to the demure, frilly femininity of the turn of the century. The world had lost its innocence and the prewar belief in a predictable, well-ordered life was gone forever. Women had outnumbered men before the war, but by 1920, in Europe at least, the disproportion was extreme. Marriage was no longer inevitable nor even particularly likely, so women had to rethink their future, and to develop a new toughness and independence. The style of jewelry changed just as dramatically, inspired by the new functionalism.

In addition, by focusing attention on design rather than the intrinsic value of materials, the Art Nouveau movement of the late 19th and early 20th centuries had already suggested that jewelry need not act as a three-dimensional bank statement, but could instead be worn purely for its decorative qualities. This earlier style, however, was produced in relatively small quantities. The new Art Deco, the *style moderne*, not only provided a focus for this decorative emphasis, but coincided with the costume jewelry explosion of the inter-war period.

Art Nouveau Banished

Art Deco banished the sinuous, free-form, ornate images of Art Nouveau and opted instead for a cleaner, crisper, more symmetrical look. The preference for organizing geometric forms drew its inspiration from the Cubist paintings of Pablo Picasso and Georges Braque, created mainly between 1907 and 1914. Cubism inspired much of the purely abstract jewelry which appeared in the 1920s. Squares, rectangles, lines, and circles were the structural building blocks in non-representational, non-figurative designs. The striking, often strongly contrasting color combinations derived from the Fauve painters (who were active from 1905 to 1907) and the stage sets and costumes of the Ballets Russes designed by Léon Bakst (1866–1924) and Alexandre Benois (1870–1960).

Figural subjects, like flower baskets from the prewar period, persisted in some of the new jewelry, but became flattened and stylized—broken down to their component shapes, then rearranged in a decorative rather than realistic way. The Deco style reflected speed and movement, and the forms of new machinery. In this it was inspired by the Italian Futurists, whose founder, the poet Filippo Marinetti (1876–1944), wrote that "a roaring motorcar, which runs like a machine gun, is more beautiful than the Winged Victory of Samothrace." It is not surprising that Art Deco jewelry drew upon the various 20th-century artistic movements. Its market was first and foremost the rich and stylish, who have always followed artistic trends.

Techniques and Materials

The earliest Deco costume jewelry was modeled on precious jewelry, but produced in new, inexpensive materials along modern manufacturing lines. So, for the first time, there was a wide variety of interesting jewelry which fitted into the budget of ordinary women.

The great Parisian jewelry houses of the Place Vendôme and the Rue de la Paix were the innovators of Art Deco style. Firms such as Van Cleef & Arpels, Mauboussin, Boucheron, and Cartier set fashion trends in precious jewelry making, and achieved technical advances with precious materials which were then copied in costume jewelry. Among the many technical innovations, the most important were the new stone shapes or "cuts." Baguettes, triangles, batons, and squares were made to suit the precise geometric needs of the Art Deco style, and quickly became the dominant forms in both costume and precious jewelry.

Square stones were sometimes "calibré-cut," which means individually cut to follow the exact outline of an irregularly shaped design. Calibré-cuts

THEODOR FAHRNER

■ Art Deco brooches such as this were worn at the shoulder, as well as on belts, evening purses, and cloches. Some of the finest were produced in Germany by the Theodor Fahrner company, which was already renowned for its turn-of-the-century Jugendstil designs. By the 1920s, the company was producing geometric Deco combinations of marcasite, rock crystal, onyx, and cornelian in high-quality silver settings. The tiny, intricate brooch of marcasite on silver with chalcedony and amonizite detail, (*above*, Tadema Gallery, London) characterizes Fahrner pieces produced in the mid-1920s. Unlike most contemporary costume jewelry, Fahrner pieces were usually signed with the initials "TF" in a circle. Genuine Fahrner pieces are highly collectible, but unfortunately numerous reproductions have found their way onto the antiques market. Some of these are so good that it is very difficult for the novice collector to date and identify them correctly.

Although this molded glass flower brooch by Trifari is from the 1950s, it makes use of calibré-cuts and an invisible setting technique invented by Van Cleef & Arpels in the 1930s. Invisibly-set costume jewelry is rare, and even later pieces such as this fetch high prices. William Wain, London.

Josephine Baker

■ Josephine Baker was already a Broadway sensation when she arrived in Paris in 1925 with the Revue Nègre, an African-American song and dance troupe that helped to translate the avant-garde jazz culture into a mainstream passion. Audiences were thrilled by Josephine's wild, comic dance routines as well as her personal style.

She toured Paris in her specially designed chauffeur-driven car, accompanied by her favorite pet, a fluffy Eskimo dog with snow-white fur. Her car was painted brown to match her dark complexion and upholstered in snakeskin. Although she wore the most sophisticated couture clothing by day, Josephine Baker appeared topless on stage in her famous miniskirt decorated with bananas, or her "diamanté-trimmed *maillot* of tulle and red gloves with diamond balls hanging from the tips of her fingers."

Her jazz age image appeared in paintings, decorative objects, and jewelry of the period, especially in Bakelite or ceramic and lucite (a type of plastic) brooches modeled on her face. All these are highly collectible today. Josephine Baker commissioned a collection of Bakelite and peacock-feather jewelry which she gave to friends and fans in special presentation boxes bearing her name. These pieces are now extremely rare and valuable, especially in their original boxes.

were used for "invisible settings," where gems were drilled from the back and mounted edge to edge on metal rods. This allowed for an intricate but uninterrupted, "seamless" surface. The technique was invented by Van Cleef & Arpels, which made a spectacular leaf-shaped ruby and diamond brooch in this manner for the Duchess of Windsor in 1936. Invisible settings were later used in Trifari costume jewelry.

Careful stone matching and setting techniques became more vital than ever, because the value or effect of any one individual stone is not really the point of Art Deco jewelry. Instead, many smaller, and therefore less intrinsically valuable, gems are arranged in lines and patterns which form the overall design. It is the quality and technique of the design which dictates the value of an Art Deco precious piece.

Art Deco jewelry was usually produced as single items rather than in sets or parures. Rings were popular on gloveless hands, and new shorter hairstyles called for long, dangling earrings. This new focus on the face and neck was further emphasized by the cloche, a close-fitting hat very popular in the 1920s, and often decorated with a brooch.

Identification Difficulties

For the collector who attaches great importance to names, Art Deco jewelry will prove a frustrating area, because signatures and makers' marks were the exception rather than the rule for work of the 1920s. By the mid 1930s, more pieces were being signed, but the practice was still not widespread. With experience it becomes easier to make stylistic guesses about dates and provenance, but this too can be unreliable because a popular design may have been repeated or revived over a long period of time. The quality of the design and technique will always be the most important factor in determining the value of costume jewelry, provided, of course, it is a genuine period piece and not a modern reproduction. There are no hard and fast rules for distinguishing reproductions from genuine Art Deco pieces, as many copies are extremely successful, but in general, sterling silver reproduction pieces are much larger than the tiny, delicate originals. They are often less detailed, and the workmanship may be slightly cruder.

The typical Art Deco costume brooch from the early 1920s looked very like its precious prototype. It was small, discreet, exquisitely made, and often took the form of a circle or rectangular "plaque." Glass or enamel was used to imitate the onyx, jet, coral, and jade used in precious jewelry. Costume brooches were usually decorated with rhinestones or marcasite in place of rows of tiny diamonds, and set in silver instead of platinum. Strong color contrasts like red and black, or green and black were prefered.

White metal was often used in costume pieces, again following the lead of the famous French jewelry houses which used mainly platinum in the 1920s and 1930s. Platinum was discovered in 1910 and its use was perfected during World War I, where it was an important component of explosives. It is the strongest of all precious metals, so settings need less support and jewelry can be lighter. The delicacy of early Art Deco jewelry, both precious and costume, suited the lighter fabrics of the new clothing styles. A typical 1920s chiffon or jersey dress could not physically support the weight of a heavy, late 19th-century brooch.

Motif and Style

While abstraction was usually the rule, some earlier Deco pins were still figural. There are echoes of the "garland" style of the 1900s in the delicate flower baskets, cornucopias, and fountains, flattened and highly stylized. Gazelles and greyhounds, along with automobiles, ships, and anchors, all reflected the period's preoccupation with speed and travel. Flowering branches, pagodas, and dragons stemmed from a passion for the Orient, kindled by the couturier Paul Poiret and the Ballets Russes, which was to continue as a popular theme in jewelry, furniture, and decorative objects

An Art Deco brooch in platinum,
diamonds, and rubies by Van Cleef
& Arpels from the late 1920s
incorporates Egyptian motifs
inspired by the discovery of
Tutankhamen's tomb in 1922.
Van Cleef & Arpels, London.

continue as a popular theme in jewelry, furniture, and decorative objects
throughout the 1930s. The love of the exotic persisted. Pharaonic motifs had
been popular since Sir Flinders Petrie's archeological expeditions began in the
1880s, but Howard Carter's discovery of King Tutankhamen's tomb in 1922
created an absolute craze for all things Egyptian. "Fashion has a rendezvous
with the Nile," *Vogue* said in 1923, and this lasted well into the 1930s, fueled
by Hollywood movies and the continuing press coverage of the various stages
of Carter's excavation. Scarabs, snakes, sphinxes, and hieroglyphs appeared
on brooches, necklaces, and bracelets. Brightly colored enamel, glass, and
plastic were used to create the "Cleopatra look" in costume jewelry.

Exotic Inspiration

The fascination with faraway lands appeared in both precious and costume
jewelry. The Indian Moghul "Tree-of-Life" jewels inspired the multicolored
"Cartier-style" pieces which were widely produced in the 1920s and 1930s.
Here sapphires, rubies, and emeralds were not faceted, but carved to look
like flowers, fruits, and leaves. The miniature carved gems were inlaid into
fields of tiny faceted diamonds to become part of a stylized Art Deco

The smaller paste bar brooches on silver (*top and bottom*) are unsigned, probably French Art Deco from around 1920. Both display the Art Deco love for strict geometric designs. The large piece (*center*) is a paste and cabochon clip from the 1930s. By the end of the Deco period, jewelry was getting larger, bolder, and more sculptural. Christopher St. James, Ritzy, London.

fields of tiny faceted diamonds to become part of a stylized Art Deco arrangement such as a basket, a vase, or a geometric design, set in platinum.

Cartier was the first to use these carved Indian gems, hence the name "Cartier-style," but Van Cleef and Arpels, Mauboussin, and many others used them as well. The style is confusingly, and less attractively, called the "tutti-frutti" or "fruit-salad" style, but all three terms refer to the Indian "Tree-of-Life" look. This appeared in costume jewelry in the late 1920s and 1930s, most notably in pieces designed by Alfred Philippe for the American jewelry company Trifari. The most valuable "Cartier-style" costume pieces today are those like Trifari's, where the carving is crisp, sharp, and distinct. Less expensive, lower-quality costume jewelry, usually unsigned, was made in this style too, and in these pieces the settings are crude, while the flowers and fruits are less distinct and look more like "pressed" or "molded" glass than carved glass.

New Ways to Wear It

A taste for the exotic was expressed not only in motifs and styles, but also in the way jewelry was worn. Poiret's sautoirs (long neck chains) remained popular, but became so long that the Italian writer Gabriele D'Annunzio called them "necklaces for the belly button." These were the perfect accessory for the dropped waistlines and long, lean, 1920s silhouette. They were usually made of faceted crystal beads, most commonly black, red, or colorless. These long necklaces sometimes had several beads that were "melonized," that is, not faceted, but ribbed with vertical cuts, another detail taken from Indian Moghul jewelry.

Long faux or imitation pearl necklaces, beloved both by socialites and ordinary women, became emblematic of the 1920s style. These could be worn in multiples at the front of a day dress or singly down the back for evening. Long pearl strands were also worn as bracelets, wound thickly around the wrist, and occasionally at the ankle by the wildest flappers.

Bracelets were a key Deco accessory and the wearer usually flaunted them like a movie star—three or four on each arm. Trifari made some very realistic, high-quality examples in which a single row of identical, square-cut, colored, or colorless pastes was set each in its own flexible link. Narrow rigid bangles were also made; these were usually stamped "sterling," meaning sterling silver, and specific makers' marks are rarely found on them. Costume bracelets continued to be hugely important, but grew progressively wider through the 1930s. They were either colorful and carved "Cartier-style" or mainly of rhinestones, perhaps enlivened with a single, larger, square-cut colored stone.

Dress clips were also extremely popular. They had been around since the

A French Art Deco scarab brooch of paste and faux pearls on silver (*above left*), 1925, shows the intricate combination of carefully set, fancy cut stones which were used in both precious and costume jewelry. A fountain brooch in paste and black enamel on silver (*above*), made in France during the early 1920s. Christopher St. James, Ritzy, London.

This mid-1930s Cartier-style double clip of rhinestone and glass faux emerald, ruby, and sapphire fruit and floral decoration, was made by Alfred Philippe for Trifari in the U.S. This piece is signed "KTF," an early Trifari mark reserved for pieces of the very highest quality. William Wain, London.

1920s, but by the 1930s they became an absolute must. Cartier patented the "double clip" in 1927, and it was widely copied in both precious and costume jewelry for the next 20 years. Double clips were the logical purchase for Depression-stretched budgets, because they were incredibly versatile. They could be worn singly, drawing attention to a woman's back in a deeply cut evening gown, or else at the front in a V-neck. They could also be worn in pairs, decorating a square neck, or clipped onto purses, hats, and scarves.

Double clips were sold on a special metal framework which was fitted with a pin back. When clipped onto this framework, the two individual clips functioned as a single brooch. Deco clip backs on both double and single clips are often flat, with small raised metal teeth that grip the fabric and hold the clip securely in place. Prong-backed clips are also found, and generally mean that a piece was made in the late 1930s or the 1940s, while a flat back on a clip suggests that it is an earlier piece.

Both Trifari and Coro in America made wonderful and inventive double clips. The Coro Company was particularly well known for its floral and animal "Coro-duettes," popular with today's collectors. Trifari did some figural pieces too, but concentrated more on purely abstract double-clip designs.

White for Night

As the Art Deco period unfolded, some of the wilder Fauvist color combinations started to fall away. There was a mid-1920s "black and white" or half-mourning phase in precious jewelry, when diamonds were combined with jet and platinum. This trend was echoed in both European and American costume jewelry. The Indian Moghul style remained a popular one for colored pieces, but by the 1930s there was also a new "all-white" taste. This was the movie-inspired Jean Harlow look: a skin-tight white evening gown, a white fox-fur wrap, a vase of lilies on an alabaster mantelpiece, and a mass of diamonds and platinum (or rhinestone and silver metal, depending on your budget).

The Maison Burma advertised its "all-white" paste jewelry with the

**Advertised as "Quivering
Camellias," this 1940s Coro-duette
double clip has flowers whose
stamens are set on tiny springs and
vibrate with the wearer's every
movement. Brooches of this type
were called "nodders" or
"tremblers." Steven Miners,
Cristobal, London.**

As the decade unfolded, Hollywood became a major influence on fashion and costume jewelry design. Actresses like Jean Harlow did much to popularize costume jewelry in the United States.

This Cartier-style bracelet of paste on white metal by Alfred Philippe is signed with the Trifari "KTF" mark. William Wain, London.

slogan, "*Vrais ou Burma*?" ("Real or Burma?"). The firm opened in Paris in 1929 and produced some of the dancer Josephine Baker's flamboyant rhinestone stage costumes. They also made very realistic rhinestone jewelry with the best Swarovski stones hand-set in silver. Burma pieces were expensive by costume jewelry standards, but of course far cheaper than their precious equivalents. They were sold in fine jewelry stores like Asprey's of London, and were purchased by wealthy women who wanted high-quality, stylish fakes in keeping with the "all-white" trend. Burma pieces are stamped with the initials "S. te B.B." in a triangle enclosed by an oval.

Much of the early jewelry made by the Chicago firm Eisenberg & Son was a response to this "all-white" style. Signed either "E" or "Eisenberg Original," these large, high-quality pieces also featured hand-set Swarovski crystals. But unlike Burma jewels, Eisenberg's proudly declared themselves fake because they were simply too big to be real. The sheer size of early Eisenberg pieces made them a precocious forerunner of the even larger, chunkier, more solidly built jewelry of the 1940s. And this, coupled with their beauty and technical quality, makes early signed Eisenberg jewels highly collectible today.

America Takes the Lead

Costume jewelry, though mass-produced in both France and Germany, was never so widely distributed as in the United States. Couturiers such as Coco Chanel were selling gigantic, undeniably fake jewelry, while Elsa Schiaparelli was thinking along surrealist lines, but the 1930s production of both these designers was strictly limited and geared toward *la crème de la crème* of fashionable society.

Following World War I, the United States underwent full-scale industrialization and was, by the 1930s, geared for the production of high-quality costume jewelry on a scale that was impossible in postwar Europe. This is the period when many of the greatest American firms that were to peak in the late 1930s and 40s were either growing or becoming established. Paris continued to dictate style, but by the later phases of the Art Deco era, the United States was actually making the bulk of the costume jewelry that reflected those trends.

By the mid-1930s, most American mass-produced costume jewelry was getting larger and bulkier. It might not yet have matched Eisenberg's grand proportions, but it was definitely turning away from the small, discreet, real-looking jewelry of the 1920s. European couturiers had been producing

The large, heavy paste and white metal fur clip signed "Eisenberg Original," is a typical example of the late 1930s shift toward showier, more dramatic costume jewelry. Marc Steinberg, St. Louis.

looking jewelry of the 1920s. European couturiers had been producing "fantasy" jewelry with confidence, prompting manufacturers of mass-produced costume jewelry to move away from a strict imitation of the precious and to establish their own mass-market, fashion-oriented identity. The quality was still there, but a new flamboyant look and a new role for costume jewelry were evolving.

From the 1930s on this true "fashion" jewelry ran parallel to purely imitative designs, and modern American manufacturing methods brought the new jewelry within everyone's reach. It was sold in every price range, and by the end of the Deco period women from every level in society were buying and wearing costume jewelry. Some shopped at cheap chain stores, others could afford the chic department stores and designer boutiques. The super-rich, of course, strutted around with their couture jewels on couture suits. The one undisputed fact was that costume jewelry was here to stay.

This unsigned 1930s harlequin brooch is of white metal decorated with enamel paint. Steinberg & Tolkien, London.

THE APPEAL OF PLASTIC

Plastic was developed in the 19th century and has been evolving ever since. As a raw material with exciting possibilities, it has been widely used in the manufacture of costume jewelry from the 1920s to the present day. But its first major impact on the fashion world was in the form of Art Deco jewelry.

The vogue for jewelry made of low-cost paste stones and base metals gave designers freedom to experiment, but there were still many ideas which simply could not be expressed in metal and glass. The physical properties of plastic are truly "plastic," meaning malleable, and therefore allow the jewelry designer a tremendous versatility. Plastic can be molded into any shape; it can be colored, carved, painted, drilled, or attached to other materials like wood or metal. As jewelry it is produced easily and with incredible speed, which makes it an ideal medium to reflect the most ephemeral trends in fashion and society. It can make the boldest, most extravagant statements and yet is cheap enough to be disposable. Plastic jewelry is sold at minimal cost in stores like Woolworth's, and even at the pricier end of the market, boutique and department store plastics cost far less than paste jewelry. Everybody wore plastic, from the ordinary working girl to the socialite.

The Search for the Perfect Plastic

Celluloid, Galalith, and Bakelite are the most important plastics used in early costume jewelry. Celluloid came first, invented by the Englishman Alexander Parkes in 1855. He mixed plant fiber and camphor with dashes of nitric and sulfuric acids, heated the mixture, and produced a substance that could be molded. It was used in the manufacture of stiff collars and cuffs, hair combs, dressing-table sets, buttons, and costume jewelry. The new material had the texture and color of ivory, but could be dyed to mimic tortoiseshell and horn. The flapper of the 1920s wore her celluloid bangles by the armload, and these were plain or incised in Art Deco geometric patterns, or painted and inlaid with paste stones. Celluloid was also used to make photographic and movie film, but Parkes's concoction proved to be highly flammable, even explosive, in this context, so the race was on to find better, more stable plastics.

Galalith was next on the scene, invented by the German chemist Adolph Spitteler in 1897. This is a "casein" or "milk" plastic, made from a combination of formaldehyde and a derivative of sour milk. It improved on celluloid in several ways. It did not blow up or catch fire, and it was stronger,

Whimsical versions of animals, faces, and fruit were popular subjects for Bakelite brooches. This handcarved American brooch from the late 1930s is typical of the period. Christopher St. James, Ritzy, London.

A collection of 1940s and 1950s
Bakelite jewelry. Polka dot and
zigzag bangle bracelets are highly
sought by contemporary collectors.
Christopher St. James, Ritzy,
London.

shinier, and available in a much wider choice of colors. Galalith was more popular in Europe than in America and was used most notably in jewelry by the French designer Auguste Bonaz (1877–1922) for many of his outstanding Art Deco creations.

The third and most successful plastic to come onto the market at the beginning of this century was Bakelite, discovered accidentally by the Dutch-born chemist Dr. Leo Baekeland (1863–1944). By 1907 Dr. Baekeland was living in Yonkers, New York, where he had converted the old stable behind his house into a chemical laboratory. He was hot on the trail of a formula for synthetic shellac when he found that a combination of formaldehyde and carbolic acid, once heated, could not then be removed from

The Art Deco Exposition

■ The term "Art Deco" refers to the *Exposition des Arts Décoratifs et Industriels*, an international trade fair mounted in Paris in 1925 to showcase the newest and best in contemporary design. Like the Great Exhibition in London or the World's Fairs in America, the Paris Exposition was a huge event, attracting millions of visitors.

One hundred and fifty exhibition centers or "pavilions" were specially built, along with restaurants, cafés, and theaters. The Citroën company lit the Eiffel Tower with hundreds of thousands of electric lightbulbs, and *Vogue* magazine wrote: "The Paris exhibition is like a city in a dream….Enormous fountains of glass play among life-size Cubist dolls and cascades of music wash down from the dizzy summits of gargantuan towers."

Anything and everything new and decorative was displayed, from cocktail cabinets to Bakelite radios, furniture to fashion. The couturier Paul Poiret showed his clothing collection from three barges moored on the Seine. He sat on his barge *Amour* and played a "perfume piano," which gave off intoxicating perfumes that varied with every tune played.

The jewelry section, called "Parure," was chaired by Georges Fouquet of La Maison Fouquet, the firm which had produced some magnificent Art Nouveau enameled jewels for the actress Sarah Bernhardt at the turn of the century. Entries for the "Parure" section had to be submitted anonymously, and only those pieces judged to be truly "new" and modern were selected. Thirty such pieces were displayed from among the four hundred entries received.

Art Deco precious jewelry was shown by established firms such as Boucheron, Mauboussin, Van Cleef & Arpels, and Cartier, who, interestingly, did not appear in the jewelry section and chose instead to exhibit with the fashion designers in the Pavillon de l'Elégance, a decision no doubt governed by the dovetailing of fashion and jewelry that was gradually taking place throughout the 1920s.

The big Parisian jewelry houses dominated the exhibition, but smaller firms were not overlooked. "Artist-jewelers" such as Raymond Templier, Paul Brandt, and Jean Fouquet (Georges Fouquet's son) made an enormous impact and won a number of prizes. Their jewelry tended to look heavier and starker than the more colorful, delicate pieces which characterized early Art Deco, and the influence of the Bauhaus (the avant-garde group of German architects and designers) and industrial design was evident in the use of solid, unadorned geometric forms. The "artist-jewelers" produced very limited quantities, but their influence on both costume and precious jewelry was huge, and endured into the 1940s when chunky, unfussy, mechanistic-looking jewelry predominated.

the test tube. He tried endless solvents, he reheated the test tube, but the mixture had hardened and wouldn't budge. And so oxybenzyl-methylene-glycol-anhydride, better known as "Bakelite," was born, billed as the "material of a thousand uses." It was the first plastic that could not be melted by heat once it had hardened, so it was widely used in industry for electrical insulation, radio and telephone casings, and autoparts.

Bakelite Jewelry

Bakelite was certainly robust, but it was also attractive, available in many colors, and easy to shape and carve, so from the 1920s to 1940s it became the plastic for costume jewelry. The earliest Bakelite pieces spoke the abstract geometric language of Art Deco and copied its stark color contrasts. Black and red, or black and cream were typical combinations. Bracelets were more popular than brooches in this period and appeared as bangles, solid or hinged cuffs, or multicolored shapes strung on elastic. Necklaces were also common and tended to be made of Bakelite pieces on chrome "snake" chains, reminiscent of pipes or mechanical tubing.

Most Bakelite jewelry is unsigned, so it is difficult to date or place a particular piece with any certainty, but there are stylistic clues that can help. European jewelers such as Henkel & Grosse and Auguste Bonaz tended to accent the chrome and brass of their sleek, streamlined, machine-age creations with small geometric segments of Bakelite. The Americans preferred a chunkier look and tended to use Bakelite on its own.

By the mid-1930s, Bakelite jewelry had moved away from strict geometry toward a looser, more organic style that found its most perfect expression in the carved jewelry produced in America. Flowers, feathers, leaves, and animals appeared in an ever-expanding range of colors. Bakelite was supplied in solid tubes or sheets to the jewelry manufacturer, where it was first sliced into smaller pieces called "blanks" and then shaped and carved to make rings, brooches, bracelets, and necklaces.

Each "blank" was carved by a skilled machinist who angled it against a high-speed lathe. He might carve from the front, in relief, on an opaque blank, or from the back, in reverse, on a translucent piece. First he made the deep cuts and then the more subtle etchings. The design was never drawn on the "blank," so the carver did not have a pattern to follow, and if he cut too

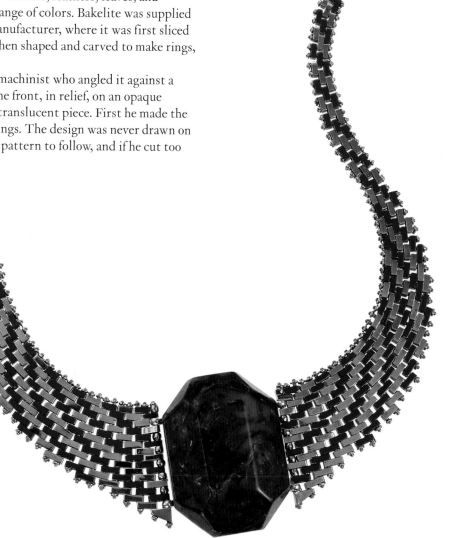

An early 1920s enamel, chrome, and Bakelite necklace from Germany reflects the European fashion for mixing Bakelite with other materials. Christopher St. James, Ritzy, London.

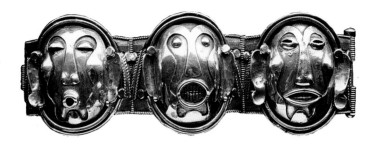

Silver "Native"-style bracelet with
barbaric masks, made in France
around 1925.
Tadema Gallery, London.

Styles from Elsewhere

■ While Art Deco dominated in the 1920s and 1930s,
there was jewelry produced in this period with a very
different look. Jablonec (formerly Gablonz) was an
area of Bohemia famed for its jet, glass, and stamped
metal jewelry components. Bohemia became part of
the new Czechoslovakia in 1918, and by the 1920s,
Jablonec was producing and exporting its own brand
of distinctive costume jewelry.

Faceted crystal necklaces were manufactured, as
well as some geometric-style paste on metal, but a
lot of Czech jewelry looks far more 1900s than Deco.
It is feminine and romantic in spirit. Stones come in
shades such as deep purple and cranberry, or the
palest pastel pinks, greens, and yellows. Settings are
complicated, either lacy and filigreed or crowded with
enameled flowers and leaves. Because this Czech

jewelry is in a stylistic dead end in relation to its
historical period it has been largely overlooked by
serious collectors, and high-quality pieces are still
available at bargain prices. The best items to buy are
large, complex necklaces and bracelets with lots of
interesting metalwork and stones, but smaller items
such as brooches are also worthwhile if they are
pretty and finely detailed. Long earrings are a great
buy, as they are very wearable today and yet tend to
be much cheaper than Deco-style earrings of the
same period and quality.

Another distinct style, inspired by African and
South Seas art, and called the "Barbaric" or "Native,"
emerged in contemporary painting, sculpture,
decorative items, and jewelry. It was taken up by
Parisian avant-garde: painters such as Picasso and
Modigliani (1884–1920) who were early collectors of
this art. The style found its greatest expression in
jewelry made of wood, Bakelite, branch coral, seeds,
feathers, and so on. These materials were used in a
fairly unaltered state for huge plain bangles, or
formed into feather or tooth shapes for necklaces.
The Native style appeared simultaneously in the
couture creations of Chanel and Schiaparelli and
their department store knock-offs, as well as on
Woolworth's self-serve jewelry counter.

This type of costume jewelry is rare at all levels,
because the fragility of many of its materials means
that few pieces have survived. Very little, if any, of this
jewelry was signed, so placing things in a more
precise context than "Art Deco Native" is almost
impossible, but it makes an interesting and vital
addition to any collection that aims to represent the
popular styles of the 1920s and 1930s.

A late 1920s creme and amber
Bakelite necklace with handcarved
pendant by August Bonaz (*left*),
shows the strong influence of
ethnic styles which were popular
during the Art Deco period.
Christopher St. James, London. The
paste and brass 1930s Czech
brooch (*right*) harks back to an
earlier more romantic period.
Steinberg & Tolkien, London.

deep, the "blank" would be ruined. The piece was then waxed and polished, either in a tumbler or by hand with a polishing wheel. The designs carved from underneath on clear Bakelite were often painted, while those on the colored material were not. The handmade nature of every stage of Bakelite jewelry production meant that even pieces which were designed to be identical often display subtle differences in finish. The most collectible carved pieces are the wide bangles and hinged bracelets. The more intricate the carving, the higher the value.

Collecting Tips

For collectors of Bakelite jewelry there are some special points to look out for. This area has grown in popularity, and prices have rocketed over the past 10 years. The painter Andy Warhol, always a newsworthy character, was a fan, and the sale of his large collection of Bakelite in 1988 at Sotheby's, New York, captured the attention of the media and inspired collectors worldwide.

Large, extravagant pieces are the most highly sought, and red, black, and jade green are considered the best colors. Muddy greens and browns have been somewhat passed over, and these, along with some of the simpler, smaller clips, may be undervalued and worth buying. Bakelite enthusiasts tend to wear their collections, so the most stylish pieces will always be the most highly sought and expensive. Some reproduction Bakelite is produced using the same carving methods and standards used for the original pieces, not in an attempt to deceive, but to revive a lost art. It is well worth buying for its decorative qualities, provided the price is low.

Original Bakelite should only be purchased from a trusted specialist dealer, as mistakes are easy to make, and costly in today's market. Examine any metal bits such as clips, hinges, chains, ring fastenings, and pins. These should not be shiny or "new-looking," although, in a genuine period piece, the Bakelite itself will still be glossy. Pin backs were originally drilled or sunk in to the Bakelite rather than glued on the back.

Design Motifs

By the late 1930s, the unique properties of Bakelite were fully understood, and designs became wilder and more innovative, sometimes kitsch but also surreal. The Bakelite "figural" proliferated in this period, most commonly as brooches and clips, but figural necklaces were made as well. This was a witty, endlessly creative jewelry style and subjects fell broadly into four categories: people, animals, fruits, and "themes" such as those featured in the designs of Martha Sleeper. There were amusing jointed human figures with moveable arms and legs. These pins were caricatures of soldiers, jazz musicians, bellhops, clowns, and even Uncle Sam. There were also lots of exaggerated, stereotypical, ethnic faces. Crocodiles, lobsters, and other exotic animals appeared along with horses, cats, and dogs. Brightly colored bunches of cherries, bananas, strawberries, and other fruit dangled from necklaces, brooches, and bracelets; all are highly sought by today's collectors.

This whimsical 1940s Bakelite strawberry brooch was made in the U.S. Costumes worn by Brazilian actress Carmen Miranda sparked a craze for fruit and vegetable jewelry, and brightly colored Bakelite proved to be the perfect material for this style. Christopher St. James, Ritzy, London.

This chunky, handcarved, and hinged bangle from late 1930s France is an example of the most highly sought Bakelite. Heavy pieces in these particular colors are always in great demand. Christopher St. James, Ritzy, London.

CHAPTER SIX

Cocktail Jewelry

While most Art Deco jewelry had a distinctly recognizable style, "cocktail" costume jewelry is much harder to define. Primarily an American phenomenon, it spanned a period between 1935 and 1960, a long time for this century, when all aspects of life changed at a previously undreamed-of rate. Though fashions in cocktail jewelry appeared with bewildering rapidity, its stylistic development was not linear, but looked both backward and forward simultaneously. The public would quickly tire of a certain look, yet in the space of a few years, the same style would be revived, which can make the dating of certain pieces very difficult.

CHANEL AND SCHIAPARELLI

The early years of cocktail jewelry were led by two great couturier rivals, Coco Chanel and Elsa Schiaparelli. Although their individual approaches were different, they shared a desire to create jewelry that would provide the finishing touch to an outfit.

At a time when most Art Deco costume jewelers were busy imitating the trends set by fine jewelers such as Cartier and Van Cleef and Arpels, Chanel and Schiaparelli developed their own styles, inspired solely by the cuts, fabrics, and colors of their clothes collections. A few couturiers, such as Paul Poiret, had used costume jewelry earlier in a limited way, but Chanel was the first couturier to feature it as the vital finishing touch to her overall fashion philosophy.

The Chanel look was based on a paradox which Huxley described as "a rich and sumptuous simplicity." Again, Poiret was a forerunner, eliminating corsets and promoting loose, uncomplicated styles, but Gabrielle "Coco" Chanel (1883–1971) invented the modern clothing that women needed for their new roles and lifestyles. Her use of light, easy fabrics such as jersey or tricot, and her straightforward but elegantly cut separates, took women everywhere they wanted to go, in undreamed-of comfort. But the practicality and plain lines of these outfits did not mean that they were utilitarian. Chanel saw that simple, comfortable clothing could be enlivened and feminized by well-chosen, high-quality costume jewelry, giving women elegance and a chance to express a strong sense of personal style without

Fantasy pastes enliven a pair of late 1950s apple brooches signed "Art" (top left, Steven Miners, Cristobal, London). A late 1930s enamel hand and ivy brooch (top right, Marc Steinberg, St. Louis), signed "H.C.", an early mark of Hattie Carnegie. The 1930s potmetal, paste, and enamel tree-frog brooch (bottom left, Yai Thammachote, London) is signed by Chanel. A late 1950s genie brooch, signed "HAR," is from the little known Har company noted for its whimsical pieces (bottom right).

Over several decades, Maison Gripoix of France created a number of pieces for Chanel (*opposite page*). A typical Chanel motif is the 1950s clover clip (*top left*), while the late 1930s *pâté de verre* clip (*top right*) is probably from a series. Both the *pâté de verre* bracelet (*bottom left*), and the heartshaped fur clip and earrings set with rhinestone and faux pearl decoration (*bottom right*), are prewar pieces.
William Wain, London.

This faux baroque pearl and paste necklace with glass rubies, showing the influence of 16th-century precious jewelry, was probably designed by Maison Gripoix for Chanel in the 1920s. Cobra and Bellamy, London.

This late 1930s enamel and paste hand and dove brooch was made in France, possibly for Elsa Schiaparelli. William Wain, London.

contorting their bodies. Chanel's costume jewelry may not have been made of gold or diamonds, but neither was it "cheap." Most of her customers probably owned quantities of the real stuff, too, which could now, according to Chanel, be freely mixed with fakes, if the overall look was right.

Chanel was inspired by diverse sources. While clearly indifferent to contemporary Art Deco trends, she did base some of her own designs on historical pieces of precious jewelry. Her filigree crosses, decorated with large unfaceted faux emeralds, rubies, and huge dangling baroque pearls, were reminiscent of the most magnificent Renaissance jewels. Her heavy gilt chains and medallions possibly derive from the brocaded British livery and mayoral chains of office which caught her eye during her much publicized liaison with the Duke of Westminster. Although she never married, Chanel had a series of glamorous lovers throughout her life, many of whom were chronicled almost autobiographically in her designs. The Grand Duke Dimitri of Russia presented her with some spectacular Romanov jewels, and their influence is noticeable, not least in her preference for a warm, honey-colored gilt known as "antique Russian gold."

"Shocking" Schiaparelli

The vital link between fashion and costume jewelry was probably one of the few points that Chanel and her arch-enemy Elsa Schiaparelli (1890–1973) would have agreed upon. "Schiap" did just as much as Chanel to popularize the concept of a purely fashion-oriented jewelry. Their designs were of course dramatically different. Where Chanel's were timelessly elegant, Schiaparelli's were zany and playful, with a penchant for the unexpected, surprising, even shocking. Dada and Surrealism were the main stylistic influences on Schiaparelli's jewelry and her artist friends, among them Christian Bérard, Salvador Dalí, and Jean Cocteau, often designed pieces for her. They came up with earrings shaped like telephones, necklaces hung with pea pods, and

brooches depicting everything from bugs to bagpipes, roller skates, ostriches, human eyes, and Roman chariots; there was even a brooch that reflected the formation of the moles on Schiaparelli's cheek.

Schiaparelli's and Chanel's costume jewelry of the 1930s was geared toward the most fashionable women in the world, and was therefore made in extremely limited quantities. Today's collector is unlikely to run across much from this period and must concentrate instead on later, mass-produced postwar pieces. Though their actual output was tiny by today's standards, Chanel and Schiaparelli had a life-changing effect on the industry because they made costume jewelry truly acceptable. In 1939, *Life* magazine wrote that "Schiaparelli and Chanel called several of their creations jewelry dresses. The mannequins modeling them were bowed with the weight of the jewelry they wore. Cameras clicked, cables carried the news to the United States, and the stampede was on."

A late 1940s rhinestone lily brooch, made in France for Christian Dior, has jointed flowerheads that actually move. William Wain, London.

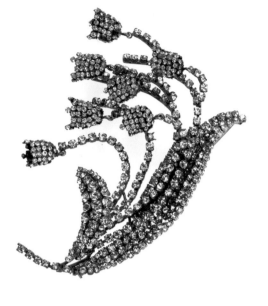

AMERICA TAKES THE LEAD

Although French couture gave birth to costume jewelry, the American demand for the new phenomenon led to an explosion of fresh ideas. The influence of Hollywood helped fuel a now rapidly expanding industry.

French couturiers may have opened the door to costume jewelry, but it was American women in huge numbers who seized the opportunities presented. By the mid-1930s, Americans were producing and wearing more costume jewelry than anyone else. Various economic, political, and social developments underlie this phenomenon. The 1929 stock market crash and subsequent worldwide depression certainly gave costume jewelry a fillip. Most people could no longer afford real gems; even those who were still relatively well off needed to make economies, without skimping too much on personal style. The American costume jewelry industry was now miles ahead of Europe, and its high-quality, low-priced product was an attractive buy for women on depression-challenged fashion budgets.

America's manufacturing industries benefited from a large immigrant workforce hungry for jobs. This labor-rich environment, combined with ultramodern facilities, meant that goods could be made and sold very cheaply. With the rise of Nazism in Europe, America further benefited from a steady stream of Jewish refugees, a number of whom had been fine jewelers. They brought their skills and talent to the expanding costume jewelry industry, since jobs in precious jewelry were almost nonexistent during the Depression. Providence, Rhode Island, the center of the industry then as now, welcomed huge numbers of European refugees, along with casualties of

A rare Eisenberg Original 1940s merman clip of vermeil silver with topaz paste and crystal bead decoration (*above*), was probably designed by Ruth M. Kamke. Diane Keith, Beverly Hills.

the now moribund domestic fine jewelry market, and put them to work as designers, tool-makers, salesmen, and laborers. With all this competition, only the strongest products in terms of both quality and price could succeed.

The mass-produced clothing industry was expanding just as rapidly, and for all the same reasons. For the first time in history, ordinary women were now offered a vast choice of high-quality, stylish, constantly changing fashion. Manufacturers copied the priciest couture styles and proudly advertised them as Chanel or Schiaparelli knock-offs. The consequent democratization of fashion narrowed the style gap between the upper and middle classes. Costume jewelry proved to be an excellent way not only to accessorize, but to personalize a mass-produced outfit.

Hollywood Glamour

The explosive growth of fashion and fashion jewelry at this time was influenced to a large degree by Hollywood and the desires and expectations it awakened in ordinary people, who suddenly had a continuous, close-up view of the details and intricacies of a fashionable lifestyle. The glitzy glamour portrayed in movies of the 1930s beckoned to the factory worker, the maid, and the middle-class housewife; emulation of movie stars became, and still is, a driving force in the American way of life.

Hollywood was becoming known as the "Paris of America," and its role as a style arbiter was strengthened by a proliferation of movie magazines, as well as publications like *Vogue* and *Mademoiselle*, which used stars as models in their fashion spreads. Stars were the American equivalent of European royalty, but they were not a fixed aristocracy of birth and blue blood, rather a variable élite of beauty, talent, and sheer luck. This element of chance, and the many girl- and guy-next-door types that Hollywood promoted alongside its gods and goddesses of glamour, meant that audiences could both worship and identify with their heroes. Dreams might be attainable some day in the land of opportunity, and in the meantime it certainly seemed worth copying Hollywood's vivid brand of American highlife in a way you could afford.

The Studio Designers

The glamorous look which audiences admired on screen did not emanate from the great Paris couture houses, but was generated in each studio's own costume department by in-house designers such as Gilbert Adrian and Edith Head. There had been early experiments with French couturiers, but in keeping with Hollywood's preference for total control over all aspects of movie production, the studios quickly developed and nurtured their own colonies of specialist costume designers, and copies of their creations soon appeared in the shops. Lillian Churchill wrote that "It is not uncommon at a movie première to sit next to an artist with an electrically lighted pencil hurriedly sketching in the darkness of the theater … those drawings are airmailed to New York the same night and in a few weeks appear as low-priced frocks." In New York alone, Macy's sold over half a million copies of a single Adrian dress which Joan Crawford wore in *Letty Lynton* (1932).

Some of the jewels worn in movies were real, either owned by the stars themselves or loaned by American and French fine jewelers, who received a film credit in return. And every time jewelry played a big part in a major movie, the factories in Providence geared up and responded with their own costume copies. Most Hollywood jewelry, however, was paste, especially in historical films, and much of it was made by Eugéne Joseff, whose company, Joseff of Hollywood, was based in Burbank, California.

Glitter and Whimsy

Hollywood created not only a taste for glamorous clothes and jewelry, but inspired a nightlife culture in which movie star fantasy could be acted out to the full. Men and women dressed up in their most dazzling clothes and went

Hobé

■ Hobé advertisements from the 1940s used movie stars to advertise jewelry, with the slogan "jewels of legendary splendor." Hobé Cie was founded in New York in the 1930s by the Frenchman William Hobé. Born of a family of Parisian fine jewelers, he brought traditional methods to the production of his unique costume jewelry, which was sold only in the most upscale stores. Hobé is particularly well known for his romantic floral brooches in the form of a bouquet of long-stemmed blooms and leaves, held together by ribbons and a flower-studded bow. These bouquets were either plain metal, or decorated with a few handset, often semiprecious stones in various color combinations. Hobé pieces made between 1935 and 1955 are the most collectible of his works.

95

Joseff of Hollywood elephant set (*left*), and angular floral brooch with typical 1940s plain faceted pastes (*right*). Both pieces show the characteristic matte gold finish which Joseff used in his studio jewelry to avoid the glare from film-set lighting. These pieces are from his commercial line. Steven Miners, Cristobal, London.

out on the town, in couples or in groups, to enjoy what *Vogue* magazine called "Café Society." In New York this meant Broadway and the El Morocco night club, but every American city had plenty of places for dressy dining, drinking, and dancing. The decor of even small-town dancehalls was luxurious by everyday standards. Booths were upholstered in thick claret velvet. Polished black dance floors were inlaid with signs of the zodiac, while mirrored chandeliers flashed as they revolved. Every ordinary working girl had access to somewhere where she could go and shine, dancing the night away in a body-hugging gown and rhinestone parure. Her clothes and jewels might have cost her a whole week's salary, but they made her feel like a star. The wide choice of elegant nighttime entertainment geared toward the various budgets and layers of American society led to an ever-increasing demand for all kinds of costume jewelry to harmonize not only with a woman's clothes, but also with her surroundings.

Movie Star Role Models

Styles of dress and cocktail jewelry were as diverse as the movies which largely inspired them. All sorts of role models were on offer, from the classy, bossy, mannish type like Katharine Hepburn to the jewel-covered sex goddess like Mae West. The only common theme was a universal preference for big, bold, cinematic-looking jewelry, whatever its style. The exquisite little Art Deco brooch just died away, because it would not have come across on the screen.

Historical movies were a popular genre, and while *Gone with the Wind* was the most successful and enduring of them all, a whole series of so-called "costume pictures" was produced throughout the 1930s. Their settings shifted effortlessly from antebellum America through 16th-century England to pre-Revolutionary France. This historical schizophrenia gave rise to a style of frilly, feminine, romantic dresses accessorized by jewelry that had some kind of "antique" look.

The distinctive style of jewelry produced in America by the Hobé Company answered this need for a vaguely defined "old-fashioned" appearance. Other manufacturers revived antique motifs—cupids, bows, cameos, and lockets. Chatelaines made a comeback for daytime wear, taking the form of paired brooches attached by a chain. They were worn with one brooch on each side of a jacket or cardigan. They included whimsical novelty

Joseff of Hollywood

■ Eugene Joseff (pictured above with an example of his jewelry design drawings) first trained as an advertising designer in Chicago, Illinois, but found himself irresistibly drawn to costume jewelry. He moved to Hollywood in the late 1920s and found an industry which welcomed his exotic, larger-than-life ideas. He established himself as the designer and supplier of jewelry for movies, specializing in historical pictures and epics. For these he researched the relevant eras or cultures, then reinterpreted the style in a larger, more simplified form that would read well on screen, as well as conveying at least a flavor of the historical setting. Joseff always rented rather than sold his jewelry to the studios, which allowed him to build up an archive of over three million pieces.

In 1937 Joseff started designing commercial lines, which were sold only in the best department stores and proved enormously popular in the 1940s and 1950s. These pieces, signed "Joseff Hollywood" or "Joseff," are now sought by collectors.

A 1930s Indian-inspired Trifari necklace, carved Cartier-style, probably designed by Alfred Philippe. These were produced in pale milky shades like this 1930s necklace of chalcedony pastes (or else in darker reds, blues, and greens.

Trifari

■ Gustavo Trifari, Leo Krussman, and Carl Fishel, founders of the Trifari company in New York, were nicknamed the "Rhinestone Kings." Their earliest Art Deco designs imitated the contemporary styles of Cartier and Van Cleef and Arpels. Their phenomenal success rode on their ability to produce extremely convincing imitations of the most popular precious jewelry of the day.

By the mid-1930s they shifted away from the Art Deco look and produced a brilliant cocktail line that complimented the myriad styles coming out of Hollywood. Impeccably set wide paste bracelets responded to the "all-white" trend, while an old-fashioned, romantic historicism was evident in the "Empress Eugénie" line, based on the snake and grapevine forms used by Bapst in his designs for the court of Napoleon III.

Unlike many costume jewelry manufacturers, Trifari kept going throughout World War II and produced some spectacular vermeil brooches, both abstracts and figurals; the most sought-after and valuable were the legendary series of "jelly-belly" (lucite-centered) animals. The collector should, however, be aware that Trifari continued to produce these animals for many decades, but it is only the 1940s pieces which command top prices.

Trifari also produced a limited series of patriotic jewels in the form of American flags, and red, white, and blue "V for victory" symbols. These were not as popular as the lighthearted, whimsical, even escapist brooches which 1940s women prefered to lighten up their austere wartime suits.

The extravagant, rhinestone-studded Trifari style of the 1950s celebrated the new availability of paste stones and responded to the popularity of Dior's "New Look." The firm developed "Trifanium," a new metal alloy, to answer the postwar demand for ultra-shiny, non-tarnishing costume jewels. 1950s Trifari pieces, particularly when found in complete parures, are highly sought-after, and richly colored pieces are the most valuable.

Trifari also produced a more understated 1950s line using milky faux moonstones or pale blue chalcedony pastes, either as plain cabochons or delicately carved in the style of Indian Mughal jewels. Faux moonstones and cabochon faux pearls were also used as the centerpiece or "belly" for Trifari's 1950s and 60s series of discreet, exquisitely detailed animal brooches, in plain gold as well as brightly colored enamels. Birds and butterflies were the most popular, along with exotics like sea turtles, seahorses, and dragons.

The firm's jewelry became such an American institution that the First Lady, Mamie Eisenhower, wore specially commissioned Trifari faux pearl and rhinestone parures at both the 1952 and 1956 presidential inauguration ceremonies.

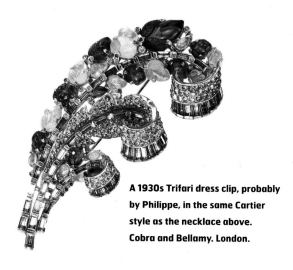

A 1930s Trifari dress clip, probably by Philippe, in the same Cartier style as the necklace above. Cobra and Bellamy. London.

items, such as a dog chained to its walker, as well as straightforward pairs of swords, hearts, or crowns. The crown theme was popularized by historical movies and by the 1936 coronation of King George VI in Britain. After this they reappeared with some regularity in the 1940s, and again in the 50s, in response to the 1953 coronation of Queen Elizabeth II. Trifari and Coro crown brooches made with deep red or deep green cabochons are highly collectible, and the sterling-silver versions are the most valuable of all. The Trifari Company reissued some of these crowns in the late 1980s, and at first glance they look very similar to period originals. They are, however, much shinier and lighter in weight than older pieces.

For all its diversity, "movement" was a keynote of much mid-1930s and most 1940s American cocktail jewelry. Sometimes the pieces themselves moved, like the Coro "quivering camellias" double clip brooch, where flower stamens vibrated on tiny springs in the manner of 18th-century "tremblers." Metal tassels or paste or pearl drops swayed on necklaces, brooches, and bracelets. Even if a piece did not actually move, a feeling of movement was often strongly conveyed by its design. The swirling curvaceousness of late 1930s "Eisenberg Original" clips and brooches typified this rococo style.

Eisenberg Originals

The Eisenberg company was founded in Chicago in 1914 as a manufacturer of off-the-rack but upscale ladies' clothing. By the 1930s Eisenberg's was commissioning a line of heavy, colorless paste clips and brooches to decorate its dresses, but customers could not buy them separately. Apparently, a number of customers coveted the paste sparklers, and, in their frustration, actually started removing the clips and brooches from the clothes. The company responded to this theft by starting a separate line in costume jewelry.

The typical Eisenberg piece had a solid, aristocratic, 18th-century look. While occasionally angular and geometric, the designs were more usually asymmetrical, with flowing bows and swirls. The settings of early Eisenbergs

EISENBERG ALERT

■ When prices for Eisenberg Originals rocketed in the 1980s, modern fakes flooded the market in both Europe and the United States. These were the first deliberate forgeries of 1930s and 40s American costume jewelry, so many dealers were taken in. The forgeries were highly competent, complete with the Eisenberg Original mark as well as fake tarnish and contrived areas of "wear and tear." They concentrated on the rarer, more valuable gold-plated pieces with colored pastes rather than the more common "white on white" variety. Your best guide here, as with other cocktail pieces, will always be weight. A genuine period Eisenberg will feel dense and heavy for its size, while a fake is much lighter. Now that Eisenberg prices have stabilized and dealers are vigilant against counterfeits, many forgeries have been weeded out of the market. Some must, however, remain, so beware!

Set with rhinestones and "melonized" carved faux rubies, this 1930s Trifari bracelet and earrings designed by Alfred Phillipe was inspired by precious Indian Moghul jewelry. Christopher St. James, Ritzy, London.

RESTORING ENAMEL

■ In spite of its robust setting, enamel cocktail jewelry, such as this pair of 1930s unsigned American bird pins of potmetal enamel, and rhinestone (*above, Steinberg & Tolkien, London*), is actually quite fragile because its painted surface can chip or peel with improper storage or rough handling. It is sometimes possible to retouch small areas if an exact color match can be found among the enamel model-making paints obtainable in hobby and craft stores. If larger areas have peeled away, restoration is far less successful and can lower the value of a piece significantly .

were heavy, almost crudely realized in a pewter-colored base metal that gave them the "antique" feeling inspired by Hollywood's historical movies. Huge faux diamonds, actually the finest quality handset Swarovski crystals, emulated the larger-than-life jewelry that audiences saw glittering on the screen. In 1940 the company hired the designer Ruth M. Kamke, who worked there until 1972 and designed many of its most spectacular jewels. She created the legendary figural brooches, the mermaids, butterflies, baskets, and animals set in gold-plated metal with colored stones that are now among the rarest and most collectible Eisenberg pieces.

Dating Difficulties

Eisenberg signed pieces with a variety of marks. Unfortunately, it is not known if these replaced one another successively or overlapped, so precise dating is not possible. It is likely that the printed signature "Eisenberg Original" was the earliest used, and would have appeared in the 1930s and very early 40s. This signature looks as though it is etched into the metal in a rather gothic, hand-written style. The trademark "Eisenberg Ice," written either in script or in block capitals, is clearly a later mark and suggests manufacture any time from the late 1950s to the present day. The single letter "E" was also used, probably in the mid-40s. There was another Chicago-based company that produced heavy, high-quality Austrian crystal jewelry in the Eisenberg manner and signed it "Staret." It is likely that this company's production is related in some way to Eisenberg, but the connection is unclear.

Floral Enamels

Hollywood's period movies inspired a trend back toward a traditional, feminine style. By the late 1930s, Victorian motifs like cameos and lockets were joined by a profusion of birds, baskets, and floral sprays. Settings were infused with a sculptural, curving femininity, but were at the same time heavier, larger, and more three-dimensional than their flatter, more intricate Art Deco forerunners.

There was a vogue for enamel flower brooches in pastel shades of powder blue, soft pink, and pale green. The metal was again heavy and chunky, but the design and coloration were soft and feminine. High-quality Trifari flower brooches were carefully handpainted with layer after layer of enamel, while lower-priced knock-offs were given a far less subtle and effective "once over

Floral sprays were a common motif for brooches. The 1930s enameled brooch with rhinestones and faux pearls (*left*), signed by Coro. Marc Steinberg, St. Louis. The hand (*right*), is a much rarer motif. This unsigned lucite example is in the manner of Trifari's and Coro's "jelly-belly" brooches. Diane Keith, Beverly Hills.

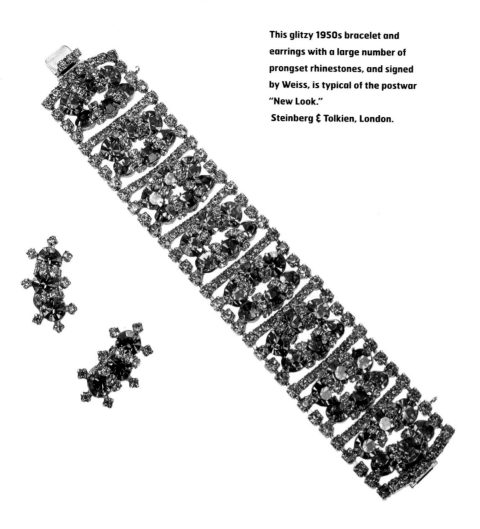

This glitzy 1950s bracelet and earrings with a large number of prongset rhinestones, and signed by Weiss, is typical of the postwar "New Look."
Steinberg & Tolkien, London.

Coro

■ The most collectible, and therefore most valuable Coro jewels are the 1940s vermeil pieces, such as "retro" bracelets and cuffs, animal and flower brooches, as well as CoroCraft double clips, called "Coro-Duettes." This 1940s double clip (*above*, Simon Tolkien, London) in vermeil, silver, enamel, and rhinestones, signed "Corocraft sterling" is an excellent example. This particular piece can be worn as a brooch, or each frog can be detached and worn as two separate clips.

The company used approximately 50 different trademarks between 1930 and 1960, but "Coro," "CoroCraft," and "Coro-Duette" are the most important.

The name "Coro" amalgamates the surnames of its founders, Emanuel Cohn and Carl Rosenberger, who opened the Coro factory in Providence, R.I., in 1929. It became the largest costume jewelry factory in the world, and was instrumental in establishing the viability of mass production.

There was fierce competition between Coro and Trifari at the pricier end of the costume jewelry market, and identical brooch designs such as hands, cabochon crowns, and "jelly-belly" animals and flowers were produced by both companies. Trifari obtained a court judgment against Coro in the early 1950s, which led to a ruling conferring copyright on jewelry designs.

lightly" treatment. Chanel produced a series of enameled flowers called "lilies of the valley" and decorated them with milky, pastel-colored cabochons. They were marked "Chanel" in script lettering that looks rather like a handwritten signature. This mark is often indistinct or even partially worn away and is therefore easily missed, so it is always worth cleaning the back of an enamel flower pin and studying it with a jeweler's loupe. These Chanel "potmetals," as they are sometimes called, were mass-produced, probably in America, under licence, so they are not couture, but they are nevertheless rare and desirable.

Double clips remained popular right up to the 1950s, but moved away from the geometric abstract forms of Art Deco toward a chunkier, more sculptural naturalism. Pairs of flowers, faces, or animals appeared. Even the non-figural double clips became so plump and rounded as to seem like organic forms. Coro made some collectible examples.

Retro Style

By the mid 1930s, it was clear that costume jewelry had radically changed, but Art Deco ideas were not altogether abandoned. Instead they were absorbed and reworked into a new esthetic. Art Deco's preoccupation with machine-age forms became the cornerstone of the late 1930s and 40s "retro" or "rétro moderne." This jewelry was large and solid, resembling Eisenberg Originals, but it combines their freeform rococo sweeps and swirls with the rigid geometry of perfect circles, squares, and cylindrical shapes. The tension between hard and soft, allied with its monumentality, gave retro jewelry a very dramatic look. This was the style chosen by stars like Joan Crawford and Marlene Dietrich, who bought precious retro pieces from the Hollywood branches of New York fine jewelers such as Paul Flato and Trabert & Hoeffer.

Retro costume jewelry was usually set in gold-plated metal, and a single, large, plainly cut stone or cabochon tended to dominate, in preference to the mosaic of small fancy-cut stones used in the Art Deco style. These large pastes were often imitations of semiprecious stones such as topaz, amethyst, or aquamarine, all of which featured in precious jewelry. They were sometimes flanked by strips or set into fields of pavé diamanté (tiny rhinestones set close together,) but the accent was always on the large stone.

Retro Chains

The retro style cropped up on all types of costume jewelry. A typical retro necklace would feature a single, cliplike central panel, mounted on a "gooseneck" or "snake" chain. Instead of the traditional loose links, this type of chain consists of a succession of individual metal strips, meshed or herring-boned together to form a continuous cylindrical or rectangular tube. Snakechains appeared on necklaces, bracelets, even earrings, epitomizing the tough, machine-age side of retro costume jewelry. Firms like Mazer Brothers, Boucher, and Maclelland-Barclay produced wonderful pieces in this style which are very collectible today.

Snake chains are usually strong, but a buyer should always check that all links are firm, because if they break, the chains are almost impossible to repair properly. They can be soldered, but the marks inevitably show and spoil the slinky sleekness of these pieces. Snake chains should always be gently coiled when stored, rather than bent and crammed into too small a box, because bending can snap them. Most breakages occur not through wear but through improper handling and storage.

Retro cocktail jewelry, with its yellow-gold plating and informal "semiprecious" faux stones, could be worn "day into evening," a welcome concept to a working woman who might go for a cocktail straight from the office. Trifari advertised this idea as "desk to dusk." The Monet company

Both of these 1940s retro style bracelets (*far right*), in vermeil silver on brickwork mesh bands, are signed by the Mazer brothers. This tough machine-age look was popularized by 1940s movie stars like Joan Crawford. Steinberg & Tolkien, London.

Part of a set, this late 1940s to early 50s snakechain necklace with rhinestones is signed Trifari. "Trifarium," a new metal alloy developed by Trifari, served the 1950s craze for ultra-shiny, nontarnishing costume jewelry. Steinberg & Tolkien, London.

also responded to the needs of working women and made a lot of plain, tailored gold jewelry with no pastes at all.

As fashion-oriented cocktail jewelry strove to achieve a more coordinated look, sets and parures became popular again, and there was far more about than in the Deco period. Necklaces were worn collar length by day, a little longer for evening, but the extra-long necklace of the 1920s disappeared. Single clips were more common than brooches.

Bracelets were usually large, either cabochon-studded cuffs or wide, slinky bands of articulated geometric brickwork mounted with a panel of free-form scrolling metal. Buckles were a key Machine Age motif, especially on bracelets, but they appeared on necklaces and earrings as well. Earrings were worn close to the lobe rather than long and dangling. Pierced fittings were rarely used for costume jewelry, but the screwback fittings used in the 1920s and early 30s were now almost totally replaced with clip-backed findings.

Signed Pieces

By the early 1940s, more and more cocktail jewelry bore its manufacturer's signature. These signatures were, however, company names like Trifari or Eisenberg, rather than those of their designers, such as Alfred Philippe or Ruth Kamke. We do not know the names of many of the designers themselves, as their identities were closely guarded trade secrets in this highly competitive industry, and as company employees, they did not expect to be known in their own right. The companies themselves did not often keep detailed design archives, because they believed they were producing an ephemeral fashion item. Many companies still in business today have had to buy their own earlier pieces from antique shows and dealers in order to reconstruct their histories, in response to the phenomenal interest in vintage American costume jewelry.

An early 1950s Trifari rose brooch in a rhodium setting. Steven Miners, Cristobal, London.

THE WARTIME LOOK

With the advent of war, austerity and utility became the order of the day, and costume jewelry was used to brighten the severity of wartime fashion. Restrictions on raw materials led to the use of new materials with the most innovative results.

The outbreak of World War II had a profound effect on the American fashion industry. The occupation of France in 1940 cut off clothing and jewelry exports. Chanel closed in 1939, not to reopen until the mid-50s. French *Vogue* ceased publication between 1941 and 1945, so what remained of Paris haute couture was produced in a vacuum. Hollywood was already in place as a mechanism for generating a uniquely American style, but movie-driven designs were most successful in the middle and lower price ranges and were spurned, at least on the face of it, by the highest fashion circles. There had in fact been a complex copying route whereby a pattern for a popular Hollywood look was made up in Paris, then re-exported with the couture pedigree still required by many women. The war removed this upper-class prejudice against homegrown fashions. Freed from the shadow of Paris couture, domestic talent burgeoned, and designers like Norman Norell and Claire McCardell rose to prominence. The search for a true American style was now a patriotic necessity.

When America entered the war in 1942, the fashion industry was beset by shortages and rationing. Limiting Order L-85 specified the exact amount of fabric that could go into any one garment. It set hemlines, sleeve lengths, and even had something to say about buttons and zippers. Menswear was an obvious source of inspiration for the classic, hard-wearing, unchanging styles recommended, and actresses like Joan Crawford and Marlene Dietrich had already given the masculine look a Hollywood stamp of approval. Fashion may seem like a frivolous concern in such dark and uncertain times, but it is actually an important morale booster, and the various government rationing schemes always took this into account.

Softening Wartime Austerity

The typical wartime American woman wore a straight-cut, mannish suit with shoulder pads and platform shoes that gave her an authoritative, confident look, in keeping with her vital role as a working woman. And while it was conceived on the most stylish lines possible, this suit was almost a uniform, and cried out for accessories like jewelry to enliven, individualize, even feminize its severe masculine style.

Over one third of American women went to work in wartime industries and were making more money than ever before, but they could not spend it on clothes because the changeability of fashion had been put on hold. Cocktail costume jewelry was an obvious indulgence, as well as a useful way of cheering up the static and rather utilitarian wartime look. It was attractive, amusing, and readily available, so much so that by the time the war ended, the turnover in American cocktail jewelry was running at three times the rate of that in 1939.

Many small jewelry companies converted their factories for the production of precision instruments like airplane parts or other wartime necessities such as identity tags, medals, and belt buckles. Trifari, Coro, and other established market leaders continued to produce cocktail pieces, but had to improvize in an effort to cope with wartime restrictions on raw materials. Their ingenuity in the face of these restrictions resulted, ironically, in some of the most fabulous and collectible costume jewelry of the century.

Silver and Vermeil

While new materials such as Bakelite, Lucite, and other plastics came into their own, the most important wartime change was the substitution of

Alfred Philippe

■ The Frenchman Alfred Philippe trained at the Parisian design school *L'Ecole Boulle*, then emigrated to the United States and found work as a designer of precious jewelry for William Scheer, Inc. Scheer manufactured items for Cartier and Van Cleef & Arpels, and Philippe was responsible for several full collections for these prestigious fine jewelry houses.

Following the Wall Street crash in 1929, Philippe accepted an invitation to apply his talents at Trifari, where he proved to be one of the company's greatest assets. Unusually for a costume jewelry designer, Philippe's status was virtually that of a fourth partner, and he stayed at Trifari for some 40 years.

The well-known Trifari crown brooch of vermeil silver (*above*) is an example of Philippe's work of the 1940s.

Mid-1940s Trifari retro style clips in vermeil silver. The clip on the right, like much costume jewelry, was available as a complete parure of necklace, bracelet, earrings, and clips, and was probably made in a choice of paste colors.
Marc Steinberg, St. Louis.

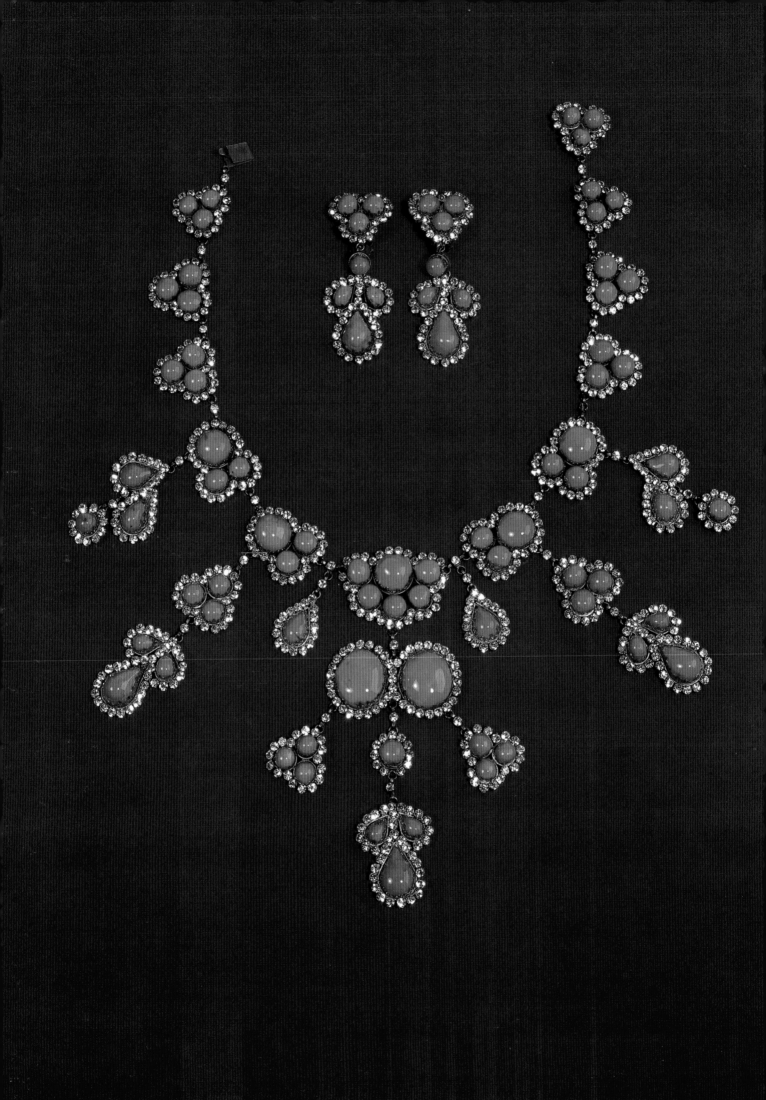

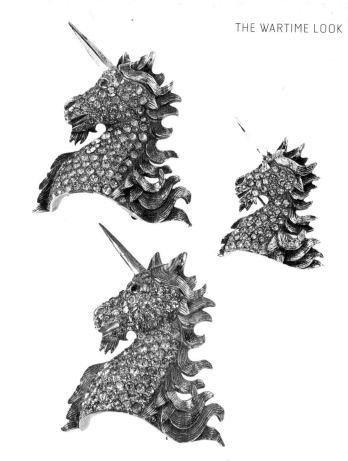

Christian Dior

■ The fashionable world had learned to live without Paris during World War II, so after the war, couture remained in the doldrums until Dior's 1947 "New Look" caused a sensation and focused attention anew on the Paris collections. The Look, quickly taken up in American mass-market copies, became the guiding principle behind the 1950s dressed-up style both in the United States and Europe.

The New Look was based on a studied, contrived idea of femininity. Its long, often billowing skirts required unheard of amounts of fabric, and reflected the prosperous new consumer lifestyle which characterized postwar America. The female body was again contorted into the exaggerated curves that could be achieved only with corsets and bustiers, while the stiffness of 1940s tailoring was softened into sloping shoulders and plunging necklines. The formality of the New Look called for high heels, picture hats, white gloves, and lots of opulent jewelry, and after years of wartime austerity women welcomed the luxury of such glamour.

Many couturiers, particularly male ones, did not take costume jewelry seriously, perhaps fearing, as the designer Balenciaga did, that eye-catching pieces might steal attention from the clothes. Such couturiers usually accessorized their collections with simple, ready-made jewelry selected from the stocks of French manufacturers. But Dior, like Chanel and Schiaparelli, believed that costume jewelry was vitally important. Though manufactured by outside companies, most of the jewelry was designed by Dior himself, and the couturier maintained strict quality control over its production.

Dior created some showy, frankly fake pieces laden with unconventional, artificial-looking stones. He popularized Swarovski's iridescent aurora borealis and used petal-shaped glass stones, marblized cabochons, and pastes that sported deliberate flaws. He then countered the ultra-modern feel of these new paste types by setting them in aristocratic 18th-century designs in which tiered stones cascade on girandole earrings or a single baroque pearl drops from an elaborately encrusted brooch.

Dior jewelry was produced in the United States by the Kramer company, and, briefly, by Mitchell Maer in England, but Dior's longest and most enduring collaboration was with the German firm Henkle & Grosse. This firm had been producing costume jewelry since 1907 and was particularly famed for its outstanding Art Deco pieces in plastic and chrome. In 1955 Dior granted Henkle & Grosse an exclusive license to produce his designs, shown, like his clothes, in four separate collections a year. This jewelry is now highly prized by collectors and is particularly satisfying to the more historically minded, because Dior, unusually, both signed and dated most of his pieces.

A 1960s Dior couture necklace and earrings made for the actress Olivia de Haviland (far left) reflects Dior's unconventional use of obviously fake stones in elaborate settings. His 1950s unicorn brooches (above), were made in England by Mitchell Maer.
William Wain, London.

sterling silver for the various base metals which had been used before. By 1942 silver was the only metal in general circulation that could be used for costume jewelry, as all others had been diverted toward the war effort. Silver was not only unrestricted, but cheap and plentiful, because the government had been stockpiling it since the 1920s in an effort to subsidize the U.S. mining industry. It was malleable and perfectly suited to gold plating, so it both saved the industry and led to an improvement in the quality of its products.

Vermeil Takes Over

From 1942, most American costume jewelry made of metal was "vermeil," silver plated with yellow gold. Faux gold was already outstripping faux platinum by the late 1930s because it was more versatile and could be worn during the day and at night. This gold plating was many times thicker and longer-lasting than on later costume jewelry, so wartime pieces have a richer, warmer, more realistic finish than the shiny, frankly fake look typical of the mid-1950s. Vermeil pieces were sometimes cast in the lost-wax method, a process that had been largely reserved for precious jewelry up to now.

Silver was used for necklaces, bracelets, and earrings, but the 1940s vermeil clip or brooch was the most popular lapel decoration for a suit, and most epitomized the wartime period. Abstract versions were still heavy and often retro in style, but the use of silver and the new setting techniques made them far less crude than in the 1930s. The Machine Age look remained, but softened into drapery-like folds, scrolls, pleats, and ruffles. Decoration was reduced to a minimum in favor of wide expanses of plain, sculptured metal. This was now a practical necessity rather than simple preference, because rhinestones and pastes had become very scarce.

Czech paste and Austrian rhinestones were severely rationed and arrived in the U.S. only sporadically, often after traveling on circuitous routes. Manufacturers had to rely on their own back stocks or use large colored glass stones made in America. These simple, plainly faceted pastes were actually well suited to the unfussy, retro style, so they were easily utilized for vermeil brooches and clips. A single paste gem, in deep green, red, topaz, or purple, was often the sole decoration on an otherwise all-metal brooch.

Figural Novelties

The uniformity of wartime dressing led to a craving for novelty and whim, so the range of brooch ideas was widened to include an enormous variety of figural motifs. Endless versions of faces, hands, ballerinas, scarecrows, clowns, crowns, musical instruments, leaves, keys, bows, dragons, unicorns, and many species of insects, birds, animals, and fish were beautifully realized in vermeil silver. Large single flowers or sprays were also popular, and enamel decoration compensated for paste shortages.

The Derosa company made a great many chunky floral brooches in the retro style of the Hollywood fine jeweler Paul Flato. Flato's flowers were larger and more voluptuous than the spiky floral sprays that Van Cleef and Arpels had popularized in Paris before the war, and the fact that they were worn by movie stars was widely advertised. The Peninno company concentrated on more delicate vermeil flowers and abstracts, which often trailed ribbonlike tendrils of curving metal. Reja is a firm about which little is known, beyond the fact that their wartime figural brooches were superb.

Sterling Marks

Most genuine American vermeil pieces are stamped "sterling," meaning sterling silver, a term which indicates that the silver content is a standard 925. They might also bear a manufacturer's mark. Otherwise, the solidity or chunkiness of an unsigned piece is usually an indicator of quality. The better brooches can be up to almost a quarter-inch (5 mm) thick, whereas lower-quality pieces are much thinner, 1/16 inch (2 mm) or less. Numerous low-

Little is known about the manufacturer of this mid-1940s Oriental face clip in vermeil silver with pink pastes and clear *pavé* rhinestones, signed "Reja sterling." However, the firm's vermeil figural brooches are superb and considered highly collectible. Simon Tolkien, London.

priced vermeil flowers and abstracts were made, and these thin, lightweight pieces tend to bear only the sterling mark. While they are collectible today, they are not worth as much as their heavier, better-quality prototypes.

The manufacturers of wartime vermeil "concoctions" were successful because they adapted to their restricted world and managed to serve its various agendas simultaneously. The possibilities of sterling silver were quickly grasped and exploited to the full with detailed figural designs. So sharply and boldly do these come across that the sheer interest of the metalwork compensates for the absence of unobtainable paste. Through their inexhaustible variety, vermeil brooches, necklaces, bracelets, and earrings cheered up fashion and met a psychological need for lighthearted distraction in a gloomy and frightening era. Millions of American women responded with overwhelming enthusiasm, guaranteeing the future of cocktail jewelry as a major fashion industry.

Signed "Pennino," this mid-1940s vermeil silver brooch typifies the most popular style of decorating a wartime suit.
Steinberg & Tolkien, London.

POSTWAR CHIC

The optimism of the postwar years gave rise to a booming prosperity, and a demand for mass-produced consumer goods. Costume jewelry was now being churned out to meet an ever-growing demand from women, hungry for a return to glitz and glamour.

The postwar period was a time of optimism and great prosperity for many Americans. The economy was booming, and war-honed facilities for mass production were applied to an ever-increasing selection of retail products. Reasonably priced cars, fashions, appliances, and gadgets all competed for the consumer's attention, and by the 1950s the American way was "buy new and discard the old."

After years of masculine dressing, Christian Dior's 1947 "New Look" turned women back into ladies. A few dissenters saw this as a threat to their hard-won freedom and independence achieved over the course of the century, but Dior's stylized, feminine look was greeted with enthusiasm everywhere and epitomized the dressed-up feeling of 1950s fashion.

Among the staggering variety of 1950s cocktail jewelry, individual styles are difficult to categorize with precision, but the lifting of wartime restrictions on Czech and Austrian pastes led to an ostentatious display of luxuriant color. There was a trend toward enormous jewels in which the metalwork became a mere mechanism for displaying as much paste as could be crammed onto one piece. Plunging necklines left an obvious space for wide, eyecatching bib-and-collar necklaces, which replaced lapel brooches as the most popular item. They were made of hundreds of individually prong-set stones, packed so close together that they formed an almost continuous jeweled surface.

These showy, decorative pieces openly declared themselves fake, not only by their sheer size but by their use of innovative pastes such as the "aurora borealis," an iridescent rhinestone developed by Swarovski in the mid-1950s. Aurora borealis was often combined with roughly textured, striped, or daisy-shaped pastes. Colors with no obvious parallel in natural stones became popular, and even lilac, orange, and green faux pearls appeared.

Schiaparelli in America
The new "fantasy" stones appealed to Schiaparelli's surrealistic side, and she made great use of them in the jewelry she produced in the 1950s after her move to America. She used frosted glass leaves and iridescent glass scallop

This signed Schiaparelli bracelet reflects the great popularity of huge fantasy pastes during the 1950s. Although this style was made in many different colors, with matching earrings, necklaces, and brooches, finding a complete parure would be a collecting coup. Steven Miners, Cristobal, London.

shells, brown and yellow pearls, polished cabochons, and jagged glass chunks that looked like colored ice. A few lines, such as her aurora borealis and pearl grapevine jewelry, were based on themes from her legendary 1930s clothes collections, but most were abstract arrangements derived from the various new stones and glass decorations.

American-made 1950s Schiaparelli pieces are not as rare as those produced in France in the 1930s, but they are nevertheless eagerly sought by collectors; prices for her more elaborate 1950s designs are very high, and continue to rise. Earlier French pieces are usually unsigned, but a few have a small rectangular metal plate signed "Schiaparelli" in block lettering. Later American pieces bear a script signature.

Spotting Schiaparelli Fakes

Schiaparelli jewelry should always be bought from a specialist dealer, because the market is complicated by fakes and reproductions. First, there were the period forgeries, made in the 1950s. These often bear an oval metal plate which is signed in block letters, but on close inspection it can be seen that the name is slightly misspelled, as for instance "Sciaparelli" or "Shaparelli." Modern fakes are harder to spot, because the name is correctly spelled and written in the script signature found on original pieces. These fake signatures are, however, a bit more blurred and harder to read than the originals. The situation was further complicated in the late 1980s when legitimate reproductions, bearing the Schiaparelli script signature, were made from original molds and sold mainly through Harrod's in London. These pieces have a shinier, more glitzy appearance than earlier examples and are much lighter in weight. They were, however, produced to a higher standard than the forgeries and are probably collectible in their own right, but should not command anywhere near the same price as 1950s originals.

The buyer of 1950s or 60s jewelry, either by Schiaparelli or any of the other designers who used "fantasy" materials, should be aware that many of the pastes, glass leaves, shells, and colored pearls used are no longer produced, so a loss or breakage of one of them could permanently spoil a piece.

Understatement Returns

Along with the huge fantasy fakes, there was a parallel trend for more understated, real-looking pieces. The revived fine jewelry industry in Paris started generating styles again, as it had in the Deco period. These filtered through to the U.S., appearing more and more in 1950s cocktail jewelry.

Boucher produced some of the best pieces, based on the intricate cuts and stone-setting techniques used in precious jewelry. *Faux* emerald, ruby, and

Boucher & Cie

■ Marcel Boucher became one of the century's finest costume jewelry designers, creating original, imaginative pieces that reflected the technical traditions of Cartier, where he had served his apprenticeship. Boucher emigrated to the U. S. in the 1920s, and started his own costume jewelry business with a collection of a mere 12 brooches, which were bought and reproduced by Saks Fifth Avenue. They sold phenomenally well and launched Boucher's career. Boucher pieces, such as this rare 1930s clear rhinestone praying mantis (*above, Diane Keith, Beverly Hills*) made prior to 1950 are signed "MB," but this mark is so small and stylized that it is difficult for the untrained eye to make it out. A specialist dealer will show you the "MB" mark under a magnifying glass.

Boucher also made a series of large surrealistic insects in colored enamel on white metal settings, and these too are rare.

These signed 1950s Schiaparelli frogs (*left*) mark the second wave of her career, which she launched in New York after leaving war-torn Paris. Most signed pieces are from this second phase. A late 1950s or early 60s genie brooch (*right*) signed "HAR." Little is known about the Har company, except that it may be related to another firm that produced similar pieces signed "Art." Steven Miners, Cristobal, London.

Miriam Haskell

■ Miriam Haskell made some of the most beautiful, collectible, and valuable of all American costume jewelry, but despite her fame, both today and in her own time, frustratingly little is known about her life. She was born around the turn of the century in middle America. Her career started humbly in 1924 when she opened a small costume jewelry store in New York's exclusive McAlpin Hotel, selling one-off pieces which she may well have made herself. In the 1930s she established a workshop on Fifth Avenue and employed a staff of about 20 to produce her designs, which were then distributed exclusively to the best stores and boutiques. Although Miriam Haskell retired and sold the company in the early 1950s, it continued under the direction of a series of new owners and still produces costume jewelry very much in the style of its founder.

Rather than cater to all the diverse fads and trends, Miriam Haskell developed a unique look which runs through the vast majority of her designs. It was rich, luxurious, but also subtle, and always utterly feminine. Haskell jewelry tended to be kept and collected, because women found that it did not date, and new pieces harmonized effortlessly with the old.

The Haskell look was based on irregularly shaped baroque faux pearls of the highest quality. The pearls were combined with fragile clusters of tiny seed pearls and arranged into abstract designs based on floral, shell, and leaf forms. Although pearls predominated, some pieces were decorated with sprinklings of rose montée clear pastes mounted in a special loop-backed setting. Rose montée was not widely used in costume jewelry; it appeared mainly in embroidery for couture clothing, but it suited Miriam Haskell, whose pastes and pearls were handwired onto their filigree backings with a technique more like ecclesiastical needlework than gem-setting.

Haskell metalwork has a warm, matte finish called "antique Russian gold," an alloy produced by fusing gold and silver on a copper base. The subtle richness of its patina made Haskell jewelry perfect for "day into evening" wear.

The high-quality metal findings, pastes, beads, and faux pearls used in Haskell jewelry are so similar to those found on Chanel pieces that they may well have been produced in France by firms such as Rousselet and Maison Gripoix.

Most early Haskell was unsigned, but during the 1940s some brooches and bracelets were marked with a horseshoe-shaped plate bearing her name. This was soon replaced by the oval Miriam Haskell tag still found on the company's jewelry today.

Miriam Haskell's phenomenal success inspired a spate of imitators, so the collector is likely to encounter a great deal of jewelry in her style which on close inspection proves to be inferior. There are, however, a few companies that produced Haskell-style pieces of such fine quality that most collectors and dealers rate them equally highly. Signatures to watch out for are "Robert," "Demario," "Hagler," "Demario-Hagler," and "Original by Robert."

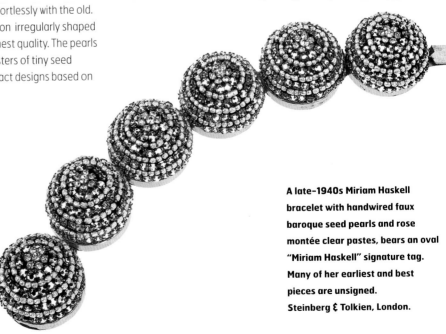

A late-1940s Miriam Haskell bracelet with handwired faux baroque seed pearls and rose montée clear pastes, bears an oval "Miriam Haskell" signature tag. Many of her earliest and best pieces are unsigned. Steinberg & Tolkien, London.

Faux emerald and ruby cabochon and prongset rhinestone necklace, designed in the late 1950s by American dress designer Hattie Carnegie. Famed for her "Little Carnegie Suit," Hattie's clothes and jewelry were worn by society women and actresses like Joan Crawford. Her jewelry is variously signed "Hattie Carnegie," "Carnegie," or "H.C." Steinberg & Tolkien, London.

sapphire pastes, either square-cut or cabochons, were Boucher favorites and were used in elegant, expensive-looking settings of the highest quality. Joseph Mazer also made fine-quality, expensive pieces in this style; by the 1950s his signature had changed from "Mazer" to "Jomaz."

Movies continued to be a major style-setter, and stars such as Marilyn Monroe, Audrey Hepburn, Doris Day, and Grace Kelly inspired various trends in 1950s fashion and jewelry. A new arena emerged in which consumers could display these styles. By the 1950s, more people than ever before owned a house, as the U.S. government had offered low-interest home loans to all war veterans. The demand for housing led to an urban exodus, and with the availability of low-cost cars and easy credit terms, huge numbers of people shifted away from the metropolitan centers to the new suburban neighborhoods.

Now that people had space and modern appliances to entertain at home, the clubs, hotels, and dancehalls of the 1930s and 40s faced stiff competition from the cocktail party at home. Chanel's little black dress, taken up in the 50s by Dior and Balenciaga, became the cornerstone of a woman's cocktail party wardrobe, and its simplicity cried out for elaborate costume jewelry. "At home" cocktail parties differed from commercial nightlife, because large numbers of people, often only tenuously acquainted, were now meeting and conversing rather than going out in pairs or groups. This inspired a vogue for kitsch "conversation pieces," both in the home and the wardrobe. Men might wear a deliberately tacky tie, or a pair of the novelty costume cufflinks produced in a variety of designs, especially by the Swank Company of America. Collector interest in 1950s cufflinks is very recent, so plenty of good examples are available at give-away prices and may therefore make a worthwhile investment.

Women wore gimmicky figural brooches for their "conversation pieces." There were battery-powered Christmas trees that lit up, doorknockers that

CARE AND REPAIR OF HASKELL JEWELRY

■ Pieces should always be carefully stored because pearls can chip, and once damaged they are difficult to replace. Modern baroque pearls will not match. Many dealers and collectors buy broken bits of Haskell and dismantle them to build up a repair stock of period pearls, pastes, and findings. Attempts are sometimes made to repaint chipped pearls with "pearlized" nail polish, but unless the damaged areas are small and unobtrusive, this technique is not successful. Perfume should not be sprayed onto Haskell jewelry, and contact with soap and cream should also be avoided, as they will erode the finish of the faux pearls.

Chunky costume charm bracelets, like this 1950s gilt metal bracelet signed "Napier" (right), remained popular throughout the 1950s and 60s. Coins, antique seals, and sealife were particularly popular themes. Most were unsigned but signed examples by "Art," "Napier," and "Schiaparelli" do turn up. The 1940s vermeil silver novelty brooch (below) is signed "Jollé sterling." Steven Miners, Cristobal, London.

COLLECTING HASKELL

■ Brand-new Haskell jewelry bears the same oval signature tag as period originals. The metal on new pieces has a somewhat brassier yellow finish than the softer, more antique-looking matte gold used in the past, and the newer pearls are smoother and whiter. However, because both contemporary and period Haskell jewelry display her distinctive style, the novice collector might easily confuse the two. New pieces can creep onto the antiques market, especially in the stocks of non-specialist dealers, where they are sold as originals at vastly inflated prices.

The 1950s Haskell necklace of baroque pearls with gilt metal leaves (far right, Steinberg & Tolkien, London) has the distinctive flowerhead catch found on many Haskell necklaces. This piece is signed on the catch, and on two oval metal plates, one hanging from the chain, and the other soldered to the reverse of the necklace.

knocked, fantasy animals, and clowns that stuck out the tongue when a small mesh chain was pulled.

By the late 1940s most base metals were back in circulation, and new electroplating techniques produced ultrashiny, nontarnishing gold and silver-colored settings which suited the preference for glitz and gloss. For those who preferred a more tailored look, classic short pearl strands were available either singly or in twos or threes, fastened with a decorative clasp. Almost every company devised its own version of the faux pearl necklace, but the best ones were made by Miriam Haskell in the 1950s and 60s.

The Napier company made wonderful, plain gilt mesh and silver-toned jewelry, as well as a wide variety of charm bracelets, for which a craze developed after audiences spotted one on Grace Kelly. Trifari also produced a tailored look based on faux pearls set in matte "brushed" gold-toned settings, enormously popular in the 1950s and 60s.

Mass Production Takes Over

As demand for all styles of cocktail jewelry swelled in the 1950s, much of it was to be more intensively mass-produced. There was less hand-assembly and hand-finishing, and inevitably a loss of technical quality. Only the most elaborate unsigned or unattributed 1950s pieces now command top prices.

Designers who preserved their handmade techniques and continued to produce limited-edition jewelry in this first era of mega mass production are the most collectible. Miriam Haskell's work and similar pieces signed DeMario, Robert, and Hagler are prized, along with 1950s Schiaparelli and late 50s, 60s, and 70s Chanel. On the other hand, there are still many bargains to be had in good-quality 1950s pieces for the collector on a budget.

American companies like Weiss, Kramer, and Schreiner all made pieces in the showy, paste-rich, fantasy style, and their most exuberant designs, especially if you come across intact parures, would be good investments.

Although virtually nothing is known about the Har company of the late 1950s and early 60s, their genie, mermaid, and dragon theme jewelry commands the highest prices, but other Har designs are probably under-priced. 1950s jewelry by Art, Lisner, B.S.K., and Hollycraft are all being collected, the last particularly satisfactory because its pieces are both signed and dated.

CHAPTER SEVEN

Swinging Times

Design in the 1960s was a journey of youth and adventure. "The Old Guard no longer sets fashion," wrote the American fashion bible *Women's Wear Daily*, "the mood is youth, youth, youth!" There was no such thing as over the top and jewelry grew increasingly larger and wilder. Visual impact and the cult of image meant that the driving force of the decade was innovation and change. And because costume jewelry was so cheap to produce and buy, it was also easy to throw away.

THE CULT OF YOUTH

The contrast between the grown up 1950s and the youth culture of the swinging 60s could not be more stark. Costume jewelry design was geared to this youthful, image-conscious market.

The one constant in the 1960s was the rebellion of youth, which for the first time in history found a voice and attracted massive publicity. In fashion terms, the rebellion targeted Dior's grown-up look of the 50s, with its corsets, stockings, bras, and pearls. The directional flow of fashion influence reversed in the 1960s, and styles adopted by teenagers filtered up to the highest echelons of fashion. By 1968 Dior's successor, Yves St-Laurent was out sketching the students at the Paris barricades during the *Evénements*, the disturbances fueled by youth protest. "Haute Couture is dead," wrote another French designer, Emmanuelle Khan, in 1964; "I want to design for the street . . . a socialist kind of fashion for a grand mass."

Advances in mass-production capability led to a continuing democratization of fashion throughout the 20th century, and by the 1960s the baby boomers, as the results of the big increase in the postwar birth rate were called, represented a huge consumer market to which industry readily responded. The profound social and moral changes which began to develop in the late 50s, and were widely embraced by the 1960s, were potently expressed by a vast variety of fashion styles which overlapped and co-existed.

Space-age Geometry

In 1961 President Kennedy stood before Congress and said, "I believe this nation should commit itself, before this decade is out, to landing a man on the moon and returning him safely to earth." What had been unthinkable only a few years before was now a viable possibility. A fascination with space

Basket brooch of handwired pastes and faux seed pearls (*top left*) by Stanley Hagler, well-known for his unexpected color combinations and large scale designs. A pair of Trifari enameled shell brooches (*top right*). An unsigned butterfly brooch with prongset faux coral cabochons (*bottom left*). Steven Miners, Cristobal, London. Enamel and paste panther brooch (*bottom right*) by Ken Lane, part of his series of "big cat" jewels which were inspired by the Duchess of Windsor's magnificent collection of 20th-century precious jewels. William Wain, London.

FASHION AS FANTASY IN THE SWINGING SIXTIES

Yves Saint Laurent

Although there are links between styles in fine art and fashion, the two rarely come together as closely as they do in this 1965 Yves St. Laurent cocktail dress sketch based on a painting by Piet Mondrian. Yves St. Laurent, Paris.

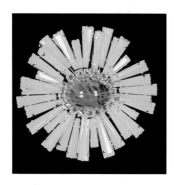

Starburst brooch by Schreiner, a New York based firm which produced jewelry between the 1940s and 1970s. Famed for its high quality rhinestone and crystal pieces, Schreiner pieces are particularly noted for unusual colors, cuts, and combinations of paste stones. Mike Sinclair, Bath.

travel consequently permeated much of the decade. The space-age image was quickly packaged and sold to the public, pioneered by a new breed of mass-market French designers such as André Courrèges and Pierre Cardin. Sensing that couture, in the traditional, élitist sense of the word, was well and truly dead, these new practitioners used their catwalk shows principally as showcases for their ready-to-wear collections, in much the same way that designers do today.

Space Cadets

Courrèges' use of silver, his all-white "uniforms," and Cardin's helmets and cutouts in dresses and tops called for space-age accessories: Lucite and Perspex bangles and dome rings, necklaces made of huge aluminum disks, geometric earrings that swung and revolved like mobiles, setting off the equally geometric haircut, pioneered by London hairdresser Vidal Sassoon, which typified the earlier 60s.

While the space-age style was initially extremely popular, the public soon tired of its harsh clinical look and moved more and more toward the almost chaotic eclecticism characterizing fashion in the rest of the decade. Mary Quant's perky miniskirted London look vied with a softer look featuring ruffles and long skirts in faded velvets. Wild colors replaced the sharp-edged, all-white PVC look, and the Italian designer Pucci's psychedelic graphics achieved the impossible: a sort of freeform geometry. Clothes ranged from the

Wide 1960s paste and plastic bracelet in oxidized white metal with Oriental faces by Selro, a company about which little is known, but is nevertheless popular with collectors who prize its dramatic, typically 60s designs. Marc Steinberg, St. Louis.

Acrylics

■ Lucite, Plexiglass, and Perspex are well-known acrylic plastics. Like "Kleenex," these are brand names, often used mistakenly as generic terms. Acrylic is usually smooth and perfectly translucent, but it can be highly colored and carved. It was originally developed in the 1930s, but production really took off in the 1960s, when it was used either on its own, for the large, colorful rings and bangles so popular then, or as decoration on necklaces and earrings. Being both bold in form and lightweight, acrylic was the perfect choice for some of the massive pieces of costume jewelry produced in the 1960s.

The 1960s acrylic earrings (*above*, Steinberg & Tolkien, London) are signed "Vendome" which was the trademark used by the Coro company. This mark most commonly appeared on Coro's late 1950s and early 1960s bead and crystal jewelry which was often sold as matching sets.

Op Art 1960s plastic pendant necklaces (*left and above*) on snakechains by Lanvin of Paris. David Gill Gallery, London.

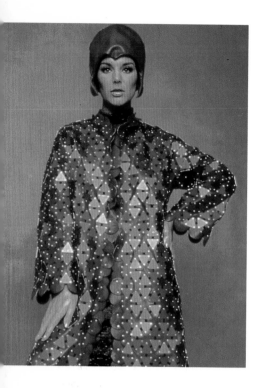

Paco Rabanne dress and helmet of metalic triangles from the late 1960s reflects the popularity of the Space Age look.

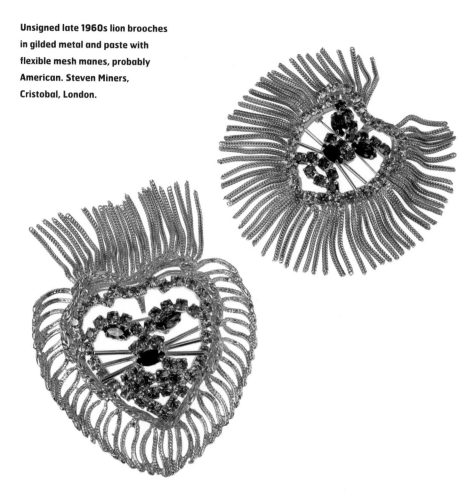

The fantasy pastes which were popular by the end of the 1950s were given a psychedelic twist in the swinging 60s, as colors became stranger and sharper. The earrings (*above*) are a good example of this trend. Steinberg & Tolkien, London.

shockingly skimpy topless bathing suit by Rudi Gernreich to the covered-up, full-length hippy kaftan, ethnic style that, along with various retro revivals, tended to predominate later in the decade. There was the gypsy look, the Native American look, the Afghanistan look; almost anything as long as it could be called some kind of "Look."

Image and Celebrity

Within its staggering variety, 1960s fashion was characterized by an unprecedented freedom. In this climate of anything goes, the search for the next big idea was relentless, well served by the ready availability of inexpensive, mass-produced fashion items. Mass production requires mass communication to create a demand for its continual outpouring of ephemeral goods. Its first significant links were with Hollywood movies, but by the 1960s mass production served a mass culture popularized by a dizzying range of media. Television now presented an unending stream of images of possible lifestyles, through both programs and advertising; global news networks transmitted instant information; magazines proliferated, and popular music sold a vast number of youthful new images.

By the 1960s, the world was obsessed with "image," as expressed in photography both moving and still. Fashion photographers like David Bailey were themselves famous, while for the first time their models, or subjects, such as Jean Shrimpton (the Shrimp), Twiggy, and Verushka became celebrities in their own right. The celebrity model has been commonplace ever since.

Following the cult of the photographic image, costume jewelry grew bigger, more photogenic, and conscious of its immediate visual impact. Massive silver Indian bib collars became popular, Lucite earrings dangled like oversized ice-cubes, and wrists disappeared under gigantic gladiator cuff bracelets. In New York, Jules van Rouge and Giorgio di Sant'Angelo made body jewelry: breastplates, bras, and halter tops in stone-studded metal and leather; in Paris, Yves St. Laurent commissioned the sculptor Claude Lelanne to produce a metal cast of Verushka's breasts in an item of jewelry. The *New York Times* nonchalantly observed that body jewelry such as this was "meant for young, modest-sized bosoms, and apparently the effect is worth the somewhat cold feeling of metal against skin."

The cult of image, of celebrity, and its attendant feeding frenzy of mass-produced consumerism, led to a backlash from idealists, who attempted to form a counterculture in an alternative society, based on noncommercial values. But even this hippy image was easily exploitable and led to a profusion of flowerpot brooches, daisy-chain necklaces, peace-sign pendants, and zodiac jewelry.

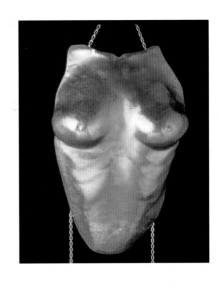

Late 1970s body sculpture by Robert Lee Morris. He wrote "my jewelry and body art are really just a release for me; to live vicariously as the maker of armor for a race of imaginary people, in an imaginary time, in an imaginary place." Robert Lee Morris, New York.

INDIVIDUAL DESIGNERS

The contrast between grown up 1950s society and the youth culture of the swinging 60s could not be more stark. Costume jewelry design was geared to this youthful, image-conscious market.

Mass production in Europe was not as efficient, nor was the capacity for it so great, as that of America in the prewar period. The war itself, not surprisingly, affected Europe more pervasively and much more devastatingly than the United States, and the effects persisted well into the 1950s. Initially there were huge areas of European infrastructure that needed rebuilding and redevelopment, and costume jewelry factories were not a top priority. By the 1960s, however, Europe was producing more costume jewelry than ever before, and European designs were starting to make an impact on the American market.

Roger Jean-Pierre was from 1947 to 1958, director of the Maison Francis Winter, a firm which produced limited quantities of costume jewelry for

A collection of unsigned American flower power paste brooches from the late 1960s and early 1970s. Steven Miners, Cristobal.

Chanel in the 1960s

■ After an affair with a high-ranking Nazi official, Coco Chanel fled into exile in Switzerland during the immediate postwar period. She returned to the world of fashion in the mid-1950s, and with her unfailing ability to read signs and portents, Chanel declared that she was "no longer interested in dressing a few hundred women, private clients. I shall dress thousands." She became enormously successful with this new philosophy.

Chanel jewelry from this second phase of her career was informed by many of the same ideas that influenced her earlier pieces. It perfectly suited the 1960s mood for bold, photogenic ornament. Her chief designer, Robert Goosens, said that "Chanel was crazy about antique art; Byzantine and barbaric goldsmithery were her principal points of reference. At times she would bring me authentic items, and I would use them as points of departure."

Together they produced rosary-like necklaces with long chains decorated with beads and pearls, *pâte verre* (green paste) eagles copied from Anglo-Saxon belt buckles, and huge Maltese cross brooches decorated with glass cabochons of deep red and deep green, by now firmly established as Chanel's signature color combination.

Chanel jewelry from this period is usually signed and sometimes dated. It was produced in greater quantities than in the 1920s and 30s, but it is nevertheless eagerly collected today. The popularity of Chanel's very expensive boutique costume jewelry has inspired a host of more affordable imitations by various companies and designers. The early 1970s Chanel-style cross brooch (*above left*) is just such an imitation. However, real Chanel can be seen below: the white metal, paste, and faux pearl brooch is pure Chanel from the late 1960s or early 1970s.

Ken Lane

■ Ken Lane reflected the period's love of photogenic, fantasy jewelry with his massive crystal and gilt birdcage earrings set with huge, obviously fake cabochons in combinations of pink, turquoise, and coral. He made knuckleduster rings with enormous jewels, whose obvious fakery was further emphasized when these rings were worn on all four fingers.

These could be teamed with his massive, jewel-rich necklaces, made with a cup-shaped or "lotus" pendants set (*left*, Ken Lane, New York) with faux rubies or sapphires in the style inspired by Jacqueline Kennedy Onassis and known as the "Jackie O" look. This look called for bouffant hairdos, pillbox hats, Chanel suits, gilt chain bags, and bold, sumptuous jewelry, and it was favored by the mature, wealthy, sophisticated women who bought and collected Ken Lane pieces.

Black metal was a popular foil for the acid shades of new paste stones during the 1960s, but white and green metals were also produced, along with roughly textured gold and silver tone settings. Steven Miners, Cristobal, London.

couturiers such as Dior and Balenciaga. By 1960 Jean-Pierre had opened his own store in Paris, and became known for his elaborate creations in prongset Swarovski crystals, which perfectly suited the more elegant end of 1960s "photogenic" dressing. Countess "Cis" Zoltowska also designed elaborate, heavily stone-set jewelry in an unashamedly fake style. She preferred insistently non-naturalistic colors, and unusually textured or shaped pastes in surprising color combinations like fuchsia and olive green. She also had a fondness for black metal settings, which appeared more and more in a wide range of 1960s jewelry.

Pulling the Decade Together

Perhaps more than any other costume jewelry designer, the American Kenneth Jay Lane pulled together many of the diverse strands of 1960s style into a coherent, original output. After a stint in the art department of *Vogue* and several years as a shoe designer, Lane turned his hand to costume jewelry design. His early work caught the eye of Diana Vreeland, American *Vogue*'s legendary editor, who loved his bizarre, larger-than-life designs and featured them in the magazine. Lane's career was quickly launched. "I had no fear," he wrote, "no preconceived ideas about what was right or wrong. I was like the fool that rushes in."

Bigger was usually seen as better in 1960s costume jewelry, and Stanley Hagler catered for this trend, blending areas of intricate handwired decoration into large-scale compositions of multiple beaded strands and gilt chains. Like Miriam Haskell's, his necklaces are often fastened with an elaborate but delicately worked clasp. Steven Miners, Cristobal, London.

He was in touch with the 1960s retro trend in jewelry, and felt drawn to extravagant, expensive historical pieces. He loved Jeanne Toussant's 1930s and 1940s precious Cartier items, especially the "big cat" jewels which she made for the Duchess of Windsor, but saw that they could be made in quirky new ways that suited the 60s sense of fun and its love of the unexpected. "I made white leopards with polka dots, and I got away with it because it was costume jewelry." The Duchess of Windsor was herself a Ken Lane fan, and started wearing his designs in the 1960s, an irony which Lane explained by his observation that "For a young woman, real jewelry is very aging, and people wonder where she got it. An older woman who has an enormous amount of valuable jewelry feels younger wearing costume jewelry."

The animal theme was carried on in much of Ken Lane's work and proved to be extremely popular. Tigers, rams, and snake's heads decorated plain gilt, enamel, or rhinestone-studded bangles and cuffs, while Lane's 60s interpretations of Van Cleef and Arpels' lion's-head door-knocker earrings remain popular to this day.

Fantasy Jewels

Other American costume jewelry firms tried hard to reflect the diversity of 1960s style, and to fend off competition from an increasingly popular and available range of genuine ethnic pieces. Trifari did a plain gilt line in textured, freeform, molten-looking metal, which paralleled a contemporary trend in precious jewelry. They tried Op Art combinations of black and white, and made a bid for women who chose to opt out of the 1960s by carrying on with the tailored "brushed" gold and pearl look, popularized by Mrs. Eisenhower a decade before. Among Trifari's most successful and

American unsigned 1970s man's lion medallion, probably designed for disco wear on a suitably hairy exposed chest. Steinberg & Tolkien, London.

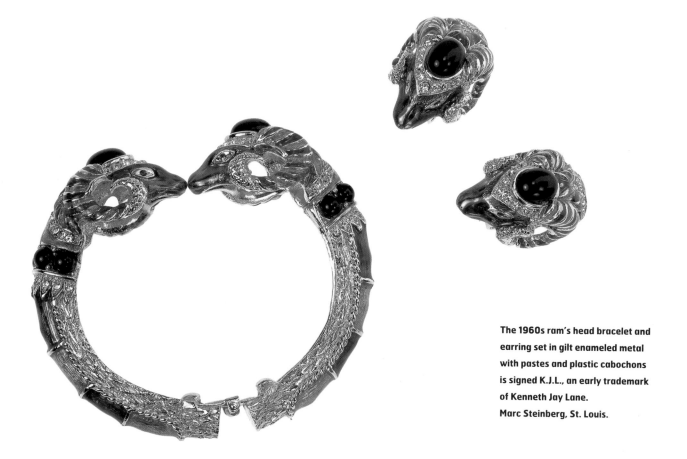

The 1960s ram's head bracelet and earring set in gilt enameled metal with pastes and plastic cabochons is signed K.J.L., an early trademark of Kenneth Jay Lane. Marc Steinberg, St. Louis.

collectable 1960s pieces are the enameled birds of paradise and the elaborate Indian Mughal jewels which reworked the ethnic trend into a more tailored, grown-up look.

New Color Settings

In line with the decade's demand for the new and striking, all sorts of unusually colored metals appeared. Black metal settings were used effectively by Weiss, Lisner, and Shreiner, and provided contrast for acid green, fuchsia, and yellow pastes. Har used green metal for its now highly sought dragon parure, and everybody used white metal, sometimes "antiquing" it with gold or gray highlights.

Costume jewelry watches became a popular trend. They were set in long filigree pendants, or elaborate, jewel-studded, hinged bangles opening to reveal a hidden watch-face.

Brightly colored enamel was used by many designers throughout the 60s and 70s for flower brooches, rigid bangles, and necklaces. Eisenberg produced a line of enameled artist pieces based on works by Braque, Chagall, and Picasso, while Boucher based some of his enamels on Pucci prints. Stanley Hagler made finely detailed pieces with tiny, hand-wired beads and pearls in a richly colored, larger-than-life Miriam Haskell idiom, while Mazer, now known as "Jomaz," did a brilliant selection of elaborate Maltese crosses and showy, stone-set necklaces in the "Elizabeth Taylor" style.

Paco Rabanne

■ Paco Rabanne started out as an architecture student in France but quickly turned his attention to the world of high fashion. His 1966 collection of clothing and jewelry, made entirely of phosphorescent Rhodoid plastic disks, caused a sensation. He followed up this space-age look with metal dresses, chain-mail bikinis, and purses or bags composed of rows of overlapping metal disks, often unexpectedly combined with organic materials like leather or fur.

"I defy anyone to design a hat, coat, or dress that hasn't been done before . . . the only new frontier left in fashion is the finding of new materials," Rabanne said, explaining his various uses of wood, leather, aluminum, paper, PVC, and other plastics in his line of "anti-jewelry" jewels. He made geometric mobile-type earrings, along with legbands, armbands, and even a decorative eye-patch modeled on that worn by the charismatic Israeli General Moshe Dayan, until it almost seemed as if his clothing had become a type of jewelry while his jewelry was more like clothing. Paco Rabanne's palette ranged from the Op Art combination of black and white to outrageously clashing juxtapositions of fluorescent orange, red, pink, and acid yellow. "I make jewelry for the alternative side of a woman's personality," Rabanne said, "for her madness."

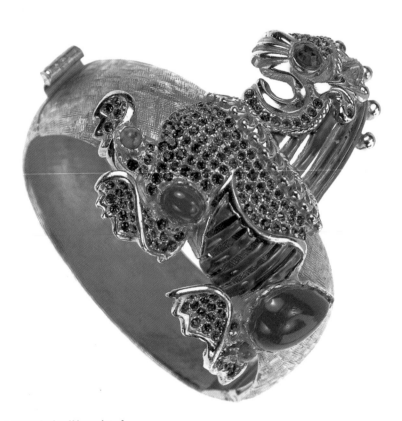

Heavy, asymetrical cuff bracelet of a stylized mythical lion in gilded metal, enamel, and paste is 1960s American. Steinberg & Tolkien, London

Coppola e Toppo

■ Lyda Toppo and Bruno Coppola were a brother-and-sister team who formed Coppola e Toppo in Milan in the late 1940s. Famed for their elaborate creations in crystal and plastic beads, they helped to widen the decorative vocabulary of costume jewelry by challenging the supremacy of pearls and faceted rhinestones. They worked in a small way throughout the 1950s with Dior and Balenciaga, and secured an important contract to manufacture beaded pieces for Schiaparelli's postwar costume jewelry line.

Coppola e Toppo, however, really made an impact in the 1960s when large, showy, crystal bibs, collars, and bracelets became widely popular. They continued to work closely with the world of fashion design. The 1960s bracelet (*left*, Diane Keith, Beverly Hills) of tubular glass bead, leaves, and pastes was made as part of a set for the Italian fashion designer Valentino.

Throwaway Art

The Pop artist Richard Hamilton, describing the qualities he aimed for in his work, said art should be "transient, popular, low-cost, mass-produced, young, witty, sexy, gimmicky, glamorous, and Big Business," and 1960s costume jewelry, along with fashion in general, met most of these criteria. The production of costume jewelry had at last caught up with its true meaning and purpose as throwaway ephemera. At this juncture, the seed was sown of its debasement, which occurred in the 1970s when costume jewelry all but disappeared until the revival of ornament in the mid-80s.

Because so much 1960s costume jewelry was hastily designed, then mass-produced in huge quantities, to be sold very cheaply, much of it was thrown away or broken, or is simply not worth collecting today. The most valuable pieces are the large, elaborate items by the designers mentioned in this and the previous chapter, as well as similar pieces by some recent European designers. Anything which strongly and effectively reflects the decade's stylistic characteristics, such as Op Art designs, space-age Lucite, and aluminum, will probably become more collectible, but there is not yet a defined market for such pieces.

Long 1960s rhinestone earrings that dangle below the shoulders. Steinberg & Tolkien, London.

CHAPTER EIGHT

Contemporary Trends

The costume jewelry explosion of the 1980s was detonated by a variety of social factors and media images, but after the starvation years of the previous decade, there was an instinctive return to the basic human need for self-adornment. The rules about when and where various types of jewelry should be worn were completely rewritten. Even the showiest rhinestone pieces brazenly appeared in broad daylight. By the mid-1990s the passion for glitz had abated, but retro styles are now on the way back. The collector of today has a rich and astonishingly varied range of costume jewelry, both period and modern, to choose from.

A RETURN TO GLITZ

By the 1980s costume jewelry experienced a revival of glamour and glitz, some of it in reaction to the throwaway culture of the 1960s and the handmade, hippy phase of the 1970s

Perhaps in response to the orgy of mass-produced fashion paraphenalia which served 1960s style, the early 1970s focused on ethnic or "handmade" jewelry. Native American silver and turquoise became enormously popular. There was a vogue for African beads and necklaces made of natural materials such as shells, wood, and peacock feathers. During the mid-decade, decorative jewelry largely disappeared and was replaced by extraordinarily delicate, real gold snakechain necklaces and bracelets, so fine as to be barely visible. This decline in costume jewelry continued until its phenomenal revival in the early 1980s.

By the 1980s it was no longer politically correct to question a woman's presence in the boardroom or on a Wall Street trading floor, and the dowdy 1970s career woman in her mannish suit jacket, straight-cut, calf-length skirt, and discreet pearl lapel pin was transformed into the 1980s post-feminist power dresser. Her shoulders were heavily padded to give her an air of masculine authority, but this was then undercut by body-hugging tailoring, shorter skirts, and spike heels, which combined to create an image of aggressive, almost ruthless femininity. The 80s working woman was no longer content to keep her head down, minimize her charms, and dress like a token man, but preferred instead to combine and play with

The parrot and crab brooches with hand set pastes and semiprecious stones (*top left and bottom right*) are typical of the ultra bold style of Iradj Moini. A pair of high quality contemporary paste fly brooches (*top right*). Rhinestone and cabochon peacock feather brooch on black metal (*bottom left*). Diane Keith, Beverly Hills.

obvious symbols of gender identity, which she then milked for all they were worth. Jewelry, a traditional marker for involvement with men, was an obvious area for self-expression.

Suddenly, faux glitz was great! After all, what were diamonds anyway but a girl's best friend or a badge of her dependence on a man? The post-feminist woman wanted the ornamental allure of stylish, expressive jewelry, but preferred to buy it for herself at Butler & Wilson, whose tongue-in-cheek, over-the-top, rhinestone designs captured the spirit of the decade by making fun of the symbolism of jewelry in the same spirit as Chanel in the 1920s.

As ever, the media played its part by seizing on an image immediately relevant only to a limited sector of society, then selling it to everyone else. *Dallas*, *Dynasty*, and a spate of Hollywood career-woman films dressed women in suits by Lagerfield, Lacroix, and St. Laurent, while knock-offs of this look filtered down through the layers of a now more or less completely democratized global fashion world. Madonna appealed to the younger generation, selling a sexier, but nevertheless uncompromising brand of female power that found expression in being loaded down with fake jewelry. And for anyone who was uncomfortable with all this hard femininity, the Princess of Wales and her fairy-tale wedding were exploited by the media to provide the option of a more traditional, romantic brand of womanhood, marketed in the shape of rhinestone hearts, teddy bears, and bows.

Retro Chic

The 1980s saw the rediscovery of older 20th-century American costume jewelry; prices rocketed as newly established collectors competed to secure the trendiest pieces. This phenomenon served both the fad for decorative jewelry and the 1980s obsession with the cult of the designer and the designer logo. Tremendous emphasis was placed on the issue of whether or not a particular period piece was signed.

Manufacturers reproduced or reissued earlier designs to keep pace with burgeoning demand, and modern versions of Trifari crowns, Napier charm bracelets, Haskell pearls, and even double clips appeared. A spate of period costume jewelry books was published in the 1980s and the thirst for knowledge about this new area for collecting culminated in the *Jewels of Fantasy* show, the first comprehensive exhibition of 20th-century costume

During the 1980s, the passion for glitz found expression in the discovery of daring new ways to wear jewelry.
Cabouchon, London.

Crowns have been popular motifs for costume jewelry from early times right through to the end of the 20th century. This crown set from the 1996–7 Cabouchon collection was sold through network marketing.
Cabouchon, London.

Animal subjects are perennial
favorites. This contemporary frog
brooch (*top left*) is by Ciro.
Ciro Pearls Ltd, London.

jewelry. Ironically, by this time, the past fad was already winding down, while the 1980s status-driven designer logo attitude was wearing thin, having reached its logical conclusion with Donna Karan's designer mineral water.

By the mid-1990s the costume jewelry craze had faded away, and Butler & Wilson's huge rhinestone spiders crept off to the darkest corner of the jewelry box. Power-dressing in the *Dynasty* style was definitely dead, replaced initially by second-hand thrift store chic – the so-called grunge look popularized by actresses such as Julia Roberts and Daryl Hannah. The only jewelry item to emerge from this period was the ubiquitous thong, a short necklace made from a tacky-looking bit of leather or black string which often sported a drilled pebble, a charm, or a little chunk of silver.

Vintage Style Takes Over

As the decade has progressed the thrift store look has developed into a *fin-de-siècle* retro craze for all kinds of true vintage, as opposed to second-hand, clothes. During the last few years most important fashion designers have looked back to earlier 20th-century styles. The 1980s power-dressing suit with its wide shoulders, nipped-in waist, and short skirt had become so standardized that it was almost a uniform, and both the grunge and the later vintage trend gave women freedom to break away from uniformity and create their own eclectic fashion looks. 1940s slips, for instance, are no longer underwear, they have become slip-dresses. A 30s gown can be happily paired with a turn-of-the-century Oriental jacket, while your mother's 50s-style leopardskin coat is a viable partner for a crisp Prada pantsuit.

John Galliano perfectly illustrates this new attitude toward modern retro dressing. While he stamped his own unique style on his spectacular first collection for the House of Dior (1996), his reference to fashion history also signaled a return to the artistry, elegance, and fantasy of earlier 20th-century couture. A freedom to blend earlier styles, combined with a thoroughly modern way of wearing them, now characterizes fashion overall and paves the way for a revival of all kinds of decorative costume jewelry.

The decade's persistent love affair with velvet, plain, printed, and dévoré,

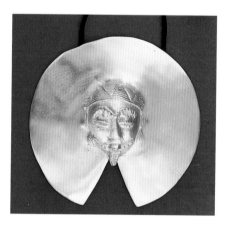

The 1970s trend for handmade-looking
ethnic styles was taken up by costume
jewelers who tried to capture this
feeling in their mass produced lines.
Gilt face necklace on cord (*above*) by
Ken Lane. Keneth Jay Lane Inc, New
York.
Traditionally set faux pearls largely
dropped out of sight during the 1960s
and 70s, but they made a huge
comeback in the 80s and remain
popular today. High quality 1990s faux
pearl and paste parure (*top right*), by
Fior. Fior, London.

Butler and Wilson

■ Nicky Butler and Simon Wilson started their business in the late 1960s selling antique jewelry from London market stalls, but quickly found that demand for period costume jewelry far outstripped supply. Initially they made copies by hand, and these were so successful that they geared up for mass production. By the early 1970s Butler & Wilson had left the antique trade and set up in a store in the Fulham Road, selling their own line based on reproductions of popular period styles. By the late 1980s they were selling their designs worldwide.

Butler & Wilson perfectly interpreted the 1980s need for extravagant jewelry, and drew on their wide knowledge of antique styles to produce the definitive accessory for the archetypal 80s look. The discreet turn-of-the-century lizard brooch was reinvented in all colors, sizes, and tail poses, while the perennial serpent wound its glittering way around women's necks, down their backs, and even along their hands. This feast of paste decoration had a link with the 1950s dressed-up style of Christian Dior, who also drew figurative subjects in rhinestone.

Many Butler & Wilson 1990s designs, like their early 70s Deco pieces, are based more on straightforward reproduction than were their 80s pieces. This is not surprising, because the trend today calls for more accurate period jewels, while the super-glitzy 80s wanted everything "updated" to look bigger, bolder, and shinier than in its original incarnation.

Butler & Wilson's jewelry is an economical way for a fashion-conscious woman to participate in the retro jewelry craze without paying the prices, often quite steep, asked for period originals. Their early 70s designs are already sought by collectors, so a contemporary Butler & Wilson purchase, while distinctly fashionable, might well prove to be a shrewd investment as well.

A selection of 1980s glitz from Butler & Wilson (far left). The firm now produces jewelry for an international market, a far cry from their early marketstall days.
Butler & Wilson, London.

has revived a taste for antique jewelry. Reproductions of Victorian jet can now be found in every high street, cameos are back, and richly jeweled antique crosses appear everywhere. The trend toward the 1930s bias-cut fishtail evening gown calls for long Art Deco necklaces and elegant, real-looking rhinestone bracelets. The lady-like Jackie O look of stiff, straight-cut dresses in pastel shades of iridescent shantung silk cries out for pearls, while Madonna as Eva Perón in the film *Evita* has sparked a rediscovery of bright red lipstick and the 1940s lapel brooch.

Revamped Tradition

Many costume jewelry firms today such as Ciro and Fior in London are responding to this revival of elegance by offering a wide range of traditional styles. The Ciro company was founded in the late 19th century, but really came into its own in the 1920s by catering to the Art Deco appetite for row upon row of faux pearl necklaces. Ciro has maintained its early association with faux pearls, and still specializes in the finest quality, cultured, freshwater, and simulated varieties. Pearls are often combined with rhinestones and paste in traditional, very real-looking settings.

While costume jewelry is still strongly tied to the tradition of precious jewelry, it has also developed its own unique history of innovative styles and new materials. Dinny Hall is one of Britain's leading jewelry designers, well known for her elegant, ultramodern designs which are sold through prestige department stores such as Harvey Nichols in London and Barney's in New York as well as in her own boutiques.

Jewelry Without Gems

Robert Lee Morris is one of America's most influential designers. His work is inspired by a wide variety of sources ranging from natural objects such as wood and stone, to ancient talismans, Celtic crosses, and African tribal artefacts. His jewelry can be identified by his consistent signature shapes: organic, sculptural, pure forms which are both elegant and bold, but never ostentatious. It is jewelry without gems. Morris' career began in a Wisconsin commune of artisans who scratched out a living, growing organic vegetables and selling their handmade products. He later went to New England where he found an influential patron in Joan Sonnabend, the owner of the exclusive New York gallery, Sculpture to Wear. She sold Morris jewelry alongside her specially commissioned works by Picasso and Miro, and it proved to be

A selection of 1990s pieces by London designer, Dinny Hall (*opposite page*). Dinny Hall, London.

Contemporary pieces (*below and left*) by New York designer, Robert Lee Morris. He has said that he looks to the Museum of Natural History for inspiration. R. L. Morris, New York.

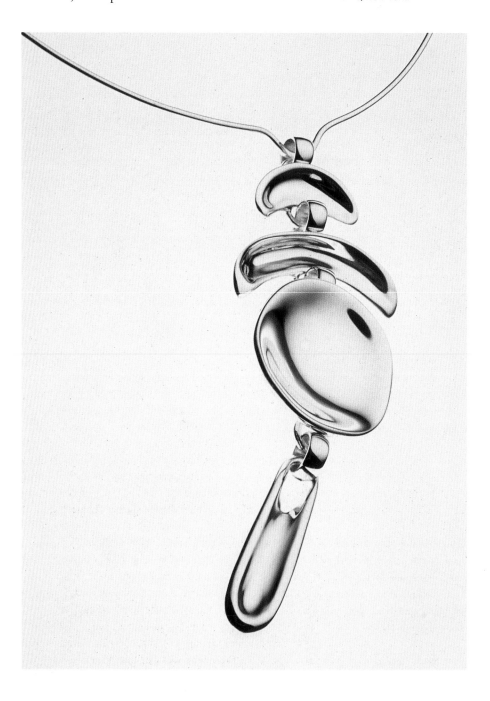

Couture and Catwalk Jewels

■ Early couture and catwalk pieces are among the scarcest of all costume jewelry, so many collectors feel lucky to pay a huge sum for a rare period example. Modern couture and catwalk jewelry is and will remain strictly limited, because it is sold only as part of a couture outfit, or produced for one-off use at a show, and then perhaps given to an important customer or the model. Such pieces do occasionally show up in the upmarket dress agencies in major cities; for what it is, this jewelry is often seriously underpriced and would make an excellent investment. Couture jewelry is often unsigned but has a distinctive, handmade look, coupled with a striking, photogenic design. It is sometimes possible to authenticate a particular piece through a fashion spread in a magazine, and this adds enormously to its value. In the photograph above, a Scott Wilson headpiece is worn by a catwalk model.

Dress agencies are also good sources for jewelry, mass-produced under licence but still expensive, which is designed for companies such as Chanel, Dior, and Yves St-Laurent. The jewelry which Karl Lagerfield made for Chanel in the 1980s is already popular with collectors. He based his designs on original Chanel themes like gilt chains, coins, and pearls, but updated them with an exaggerated mid-80s flashiness, then tapped into the period's designer mania by emblazoning the pieces with the now famous "CC" logo.

enormously successful. By 1977 Morris established his own New York gallery, Artwear, and used it to showcase the work of a number of experimental jewelry designers. They tended to shun the traditional vocabulary of jewelry design and focused on new materials like rubber and silicone, silk, wood, granites, resins, bronze, and copper.

After a ten year collaboration with Donna Karan, Morris established his own company in 1992, and this has become successful worldwide. However, the prototype for each and every piece sold under the RLM trademark is actually designed by Robert Lee Morris himself, rather than a team of inhouse designers which is the usual practice in most large jewelry firms.

Network Marketing

Innovations in the style of contemporary costume jewelry have been mirrored by some changes in the way that it is sold. Department stores and boutiques are still important outlets, but they face competition from new venues like airport duty-free schemes and cable TV mail order shopping channels. A great deal of costume jewelry today now changes hands through network marketing, which means that pieces are not sold in stores but by a team of independent distributors, usually women, who work part time selling

During the designer craze of the 1980s, the "CC" logo reigned supreme. Plastic and gilt earrings by Karl Lagerfeld for Chanel. Steinberg & Tolkien, London.

Iradj Moini

■ Iradj Moini's truly striking and dramatic jewelry tends to center on huge, decorative brooches. These are made up from a mosaic of large colored glass pastes, mostly unfaceted, and individually handset in fragile wire frames. The handmade nature of his jewelry means that an Iradj Moini piece may take up to two full weeks to complete.

His work appeals on two levels simultaneously. The figurative subject of an Iradj brooch is in itself interesting, ranging from elephant heads, parrots, motorcycles, apples, pears, and floral bouquets to the creepiest, crawliest crustaceans imaginable. The above 1990s lobster brooch with articulated claws is a typical Iradj piece. His sense of each of these subjects is conveyed by both his linear design and his inspired array of irregularly shaped and colored pastes.

Because it is handmade, no two pieces of Iradj Moini jewelry are exactly the same, and even earrings sold as a pair will display some subtle difference from each other. Contemporary Iradj jewelry is very expensive, but so popular with today's collectors and costume jewelry enthusiasts worldwide that his newest designs immediately become collectibles.

products through personal contacts, crafts fairs, bazaars, and parties at home. The idea is that the distributor, as a free agent, benefits from complete job flexibility, while the product itself can be offered at a highly competitive price because retail overheads and staff salaries have been eliminated. Most of this type of jewelry is simply bought in from overseas manufacturers, but the Caura company has specially commissioned the well-known jewelry designer Eric van Peterson to work on selected lines. Van Peterson's Caura pieces, particularly those which he has designed around historical themes, are both attractive and an excellent deal. This type of network jewelry may well have collectible potential in the future.

Another over the top piece of insect glitz from the collection of Diane Keith, Beverly Hills.

Fior

■ Fior in London is famed for its high quality costume jewelry, which looks so realistic that Elizabeth Taylor once commissioned the firm to produce an exact copy of one of her spectacular precious jewels. The company was established in 1892 by the Feldman family, who still own and operate Fior today. They started off specializing in precious jewelry, but by the late 1920s switched to costume in response to the Art Deco craze for fabulous fakes. In 1956 Fior was granted a Royal Warrant by Prince Bernhard of the Netherlands, the first costume jewelry company to receive such an honor.

The Feldmans are among a tiny handful of manufacturers to anticipate a future interest in their product; they kept back special pieces over the course of the last 50 years and these now form one of the most interesting and comprehensive archives of 20th-century costume jewelry. Fior's business today is centered on its two London shops, each an Aladdin's cave of sparkling jewels. While their earliest pieces were unsigned, their exclusive lines of specially commissioned contemporary designs now bear the Fior name. These look set to become some of the most desirable collectibles of the future. The above pearl and paste choker and bracelet is a fine example of Fior's contemporary work.

Crosses remain a popular subject for costume jewelry in the 1990s. This set was designed by Eric van Peterson for the Caura collection.

Junk versus Quality

Modern manufacturing techniques have led to the proliferation of very poor quality costume jewelry which is worn for the brief duration of each passing fad, then quite rightly, thrown away. However, better quality pieces, in terms of design and technique, will probably rise in value over the next few decades and should be kept. As with most future antiques, collectible potential is most often tied to the original sale price, so top-of-the-line costume jewelry will always be your best bet in terms of investment. But investment alone will never be the point of this fascinating area of collecting.

Costume jewelry in the late 1990s is making a major comeback because, as it has always done, it proves to be the perfect way to personalize an outfit and express the wearer's own sense of style. In the atmosphere of retro chic, personal style is everything. It is up to you to make your own selections and combinations, and there is only one rule: wear and enjoy!

Glossary

aigrette
1. A plume-shaped ornament worn in a hat or directly on the head. 2. A spray of feather-shaped gems.

alloy
A combination of two or more metals.

articulated, movable.
Connected with flexible joints or segments. Often used to refer to bracelets which can bend, unlike cuff or bangle bracelets, which are rigid.

baguette
A narrow, rectangulargem or paste.

bangle
A rigid, circular, or oval bracelet that slips over the hand.

Baroque pearl
A bumpy, irregularly shaped pearl; faux versions were used in Miriam Haskell costume jewelry.

bog oak
Fossilized peat used mainly in 19th-century Irish costume jewelry.

book chain
Necklace with square or rectangular links that was popular in the 19th century.

brooch
An alternative name for a pin.

cabochon
A smooth, unfaceted, dome-like gem or paste with a flat back.

calibré
Small faceted gems or pastes specially cut to fit the contours of a particular setting.

chain mail
Mesh of tiny metal plates or rings woven together to form a metal fabric particularly popular in costume jewelry in the 1960s.

chatelaine
1. Originally, a brooch or hook worn at the waist from which a watch, purse, scissors, keys, or other useful items could be suspended. 2. Later, a purely decorative pair of brooches attached by a chain.

circa
Used when precise dating is not possible, but generally means made within ten years of date given.

crystal
Glass of the highest quality, made from a mixture of quartz, sand, soda, potash, and lead oxide, heated to 1500 degrees centigrade, resulting in a substance very like natural, or rock, crystal.

cut steel
Tiny, faceted steel studs used in early costume jewelry. See marcasite.

dog collar
A wide choker-type necklace popular in the 1960s, and before that in Victorian times.

double clip
A pair of clips mounted on a detachable pinback mechanism so that the clips can be worn together as one brooch, or separately as two clips.

en tremblant
An item of jewelry with a motif (usually a flower or insect) that is mounted on a tiny spring so that it trembles with the wearer's movements. Also called "tremblers" or "nodders."

estate jewelry
Previously owned jewelry which may be antique or vintage, but can also be modern.

essence d'Orient
A fish-scale coating used on glass or plastic beads to create faux pearls.

facets
Cuts made to the surface of a gem or paste which make it glitter by reflecting light.

filigree
Intricate metal decoration created by twisting thin wires into lacelike patterns.

findings
A broad term used to refer to the functional parts of jewelry such as catches, clasps, clips, jump rings, chains, etc.

foiled back
Reflective metal coating or thin sheet of metal placed behind a gem or paste to enhance the shine or color.

French jet
Shiny black glass imitating true jet.

German silver
An alloy of nickel, copper, and zinc, also known as nickel silver.

gilding
Process where base metal is plated with a thin layer of gold.

girandole
Jewelry design of three separate drops suspended from a central stone or motif.

granulation
A gold-working technique in which a metal surface is decorated with grains of gold.

jabot pin
A long stick pin with decorative motifs at the top and bottom.

jet
Fossilized coal widely used in the 19th century for mourning jewelry.

lavallière
A necklace with a single stone or pendant suspended from it.

loupe
Magnifying lens used by jewelers.

Lucite
Dupont trade name for acrylic plastic.

marcasite
Iron pyrites gemstones which share their silvery metallic luster and are often confused with cut steel,. Marcasites were used extensively in the 1920s and 1930s, and often set in silver.

marquise cut
An oval-shaped gem or paste that is pointed at both ends.

matinee-length
A single-strand necklace measuring 24–36in (60–90cm).

mourning jewelry
Worn to commemorate a deceased loved one. Often made of jet and sometimes containing a lock of hair from the deceased.

opera-length
An especially long, single-strand necklace measuring 4-41/2 feet (120–130cm), and sometimes extending to 10 feet (3m).

painted enamel
Process in which enamel is applied as a liquid rather than as a powder and then baked at a lower temperatures than that used in firing powdered enamels. Used extensively on American costume jewelry of the 1930s and 1940s.

parure
A matching set or suite of jewelry such as necklace, bracelet, brooch, and earrings. A demi-parure is two matched pieces such as brooch and earrings.

paste
Crystal or ordinary glass with a high lead content that has been cut to resemble a gemstone. Also known as Stras or diamanté in Europe and rhinestone in America. See **crystal.**

pate-de-verre
A paste of crushed glass colored with metal oxides and then molded and fired. Used notably in early Chanel jewelry. Also called poured glass.

patina
The coloration which occurs on some metals when they are exposed to the atmosphere over time. This can be desirable on costume jewelry as it helps to distinguish originals from modern pieces.

pavé
Many gems or pastes set very close together (literally paved) so the effect is one of a continuous, jeweled surface.

pietra dura
Mosaic of small flat stones that form a scene or picture.

pinchbeck
A metal alloy of copper and zinc developed in the 18th century to imitate gold.

pot metal
A greyish base metal made from an alloy of tin and lead used extensively in early 20th-century costume jewelry. Notable are the pot metal flowers and animals that were made in America for Chanel.

prong set
Pastes held in place by four, clawlike metal prongs bending over their surface.

regard ring
Ring set with a strip of gems, the first letter of which spells out "REGARD" (Ruby, Emerald, Garnet, Amethyst, Ruby, Diamond.)

rhinestone
Faceted glass much used in costume jewelry; can be colorless or colored with a light-reflecting foil backing. See **paste, foiled back.**

rock crystal
A colorless quartz that is much harder than and often used in Art Deco jewelry, See **crystal.**

rose montée
A faceted, flat-backed paste often mounted in a pierced-metal, cup setting ready for wiring on to jewelry or clothing.

sautoir
A very long necklace made of beads or pearls and often terminating in a tassel or pendant; very popular in the 1920s.

scatter pin
A tiny, often animal-themed pin, sometimes worn in groups, and popular in the 1950s, .

screwback
An earring fitting for non-pierced ears, usually indicative of an earlier date than the more modern, clip-back fitting.

seed pearl
Either a real or artificial pearl which weighs less than one quarter of a gram.

signed
A piece which is either engraved, stamped, or impressed with a name, trademark, symbol, initials, indicating the designer or manufacturer.

solder
A metal alloy melted to fuse pieces of jewelry together, often used in the repair of costume jewelry.

spacer
A decorative bead used mainly on necklaces to set off and separate larger beads or pearls.

stamping
1. A process where a die or hammer is used to make decorative textures on metal.
2. Prepared jewelry components which are assembled into finished pieces.

sterling silver
Alloy that is 92.5 percent pure silver and 7.5 percent base metal such as copper.

stickpin
A straight pin ornamented on the top and usually worn on a scarf or tie. See **jabot.**

stonecutting techniques
The various procedures which are used to prepare a raw gem for setting in a piece of jewelry, such as faceting, cutting, polishing, and grinding. Costume jewelry designs often mirror new techniques.

Trifarium
An ultra-shiny, nontarnishing, metal alloy patented by the Trifari company and used in its costume jewelry.

vermeil
Sterling silver plated with gold. Also called silver gilt or gold wash.

Vulcanite
A very hard rubber produced in the 19th century to imitate jet and used for mourning jewelry.

ziggurat
Stepped triangle or pyramid shape that became a favorite Art Deco motif.

Index